WHAT EMPLOYERS WANT

WHAT EMPLOYERS WANT

Job Prospects for Less-Educated Workers

Harry J. Holzer

RUSSELL SAGE FOUNDATION / NEW YORK

The Russell Sage Foundation

The Russell Sage Foundation, one of the oldest of America's general purpose foundations, was established in 1907 by Mrs. Margaret Olivia Sage for "the improvement of social and living conditions in the United States." The Foundation seeks to fulfill this mandate by fostering the development and dissemination of knowledge about the country's political, social, and economic problems. While the Foundation endeavors to assure the accuracy and objectivity of each book it publishes, the conclusions and interpretations in Russell Sage Foundation publications are those of the authors and not of the Foundation, its Trustees, or its staff. Publication by Russell Sage, therefore, does not imply Foundation endorsement.

Library of Congress Cataloging-in-Publication Data

Holzer, Harry J., 1957-
What employers want: job prospects for less-educated workers / Harry J. Holzer.
p. cm.
Includes bibliographical references and index.
ISBN 0-87154-391-5 (hardbound)
1. Unskilled labor—Supply and demand—United States. 2. Skilled labor—Supply and demand—United States. 3. Labor supply—Effect of education on—United States. I. Title.
HD5724.H578 1996
331.11'422—dc20 95-23154
CIP

The paper used in this publication meets the minimum requirements of American National Standard for Information Sciences—Permanence of Paper for Printed Library Materials, ANSI Z39.48-1992.

Text design by John Johnston.

RUSSELL SAGE FOUNDATION
112 East 64th Street, New York, New York 10021

10 9 8 7 6 5 4 3 2 1

Contents

Acknowledgments

I would like to thank the Russell Sage Foundation, and especially the foundation's president, Eric Wanner, for generous financial support for the collection of the data on which this study is based. I am also grateful for the additional support provided by the Ford Foundation and the director of its Urban Poverty program, Robert Curvin. And I appreciate the helpful comments and the support of the members of the Multi-City Study of Urban Inequality, especially Sheldon Danziger and Keith Ihlanfeldt.

The survey of employers on which this study is based was capably administered by the Survey Research Division of the Institute for Public Policy and Social Research at Michigan State University. I wish to thank the staff members of the institute, particularly project managers Renee DeGroot and Karen Clark, for their hard work and perseverance throughout a difficult project.

Several graduate students of the Economics Department at Michigan State University also assisted me at various stages of the administration of the household survey and in the research for this volume. They include Kelly Hallman, Scott Baier, Jennifer Tracey, Raul Tomas, Marianne Johnson, and Jess Reaser. I thank them for their efforts and for their contributions to this work.

I would also like to thank seminar participants at the U.S. Department of Health and Human Services and at Harvard University, Western Michigan University, Northwestern University, and the University of Chicago for their helpful comments. Eric Wanner, David Haproff, Philip Harvey, and Jeffrey Zax also provided useful suggestions.

Last, I would like to thank my wife, Deborah Shulman, and my daughter Simone for their loving support during the whole of this project.

Preface

This monograph presents the results of a survey of employers in four major metropolitan areas in the United States. The survey, funded by the Russell Sage Foundation, was administered to 800 employers in each metropolitan area as part of the Multi-City Study of Urban Inequality. The aim of the broader project, funded by the Russell Sage and Ford Foundations, was to analyze the interactions of racial attitudes and behavior in the housing and labor markets of Atlanta, Boston, Detroit, and Los Angeles.

The employer survey was designed to enhance our understanding of the *demand* side of the labor market that less-educated workers currently face—in other words, the nature and characteristics of the jobs they fill and of the employers who hire them, and how these factors influence which workers get hired and what they are paid. In this study, I focused particularly on the market for less-educated minority workers, especially for those who reside in the central cities of four metropolitan areas.

The results of the survey shed new light on a variety of hypotheses that have been developed by social scientists to explain the problems of less-educated workers, especially minorities, in recent years. I also hope the results will contribute to the discussion of policy options for improving the employment and earnings prospects of these workers.

1 / Introduction

This study of employers and jobs for less-educated workers in the United States begins with a review of recent labor market developments for minorities and less-educated workers. It continues with a discussion of various aspects of the employer survey administered as part of the Multi-City Study of Urban Inequality, reviewing in some detail the geographic, economic, and social characteristics of the four metropolitan areas in which the survey was administered, and also various sampling issues that bear on the representativeness of the employers and jobs that appear in the survey. The chapter concludes with a summary of the study's principal findings.

RECENT LABOR MARKET TRENDS AND THEIR CAUSES

The labor market situation of less-educated minorities, especially young African Americans in inner-city areas, is grim. Their employment rates have deteriorated dramatically over the past two decades, and the gains in relative earnings achieved during the 1960s and early 1970s (due to improvements in educational attainments, federal antidiscrimination efforts, and the like) began to erode in the 1980s.[1]

A number of hypotheses have been developed in recent years to explain these trends. These hypotheses include the growing demand for skills, deindustrialization, relocation of employers, and racial discrimination.

1) Growing Employer Demand for Skills. The labor market situation of inner-city minorities does appear to be related to a more general deterioration in the market for less-educated workers in the United States. Young male high school graduates and dropouts of all races now earn 20–30 percent less per hour than such workers did in the early 1970s, and they work (and participate in the labor force) less frequently as well.

A large body of economic research shows that, among other things, there was a marked shift in employer hiring away from less-educated toward more-educated workers during this time period. The reasons for this shift are not totally clear, though technological advances and rising import competition seem to be among them.[2]

Even in jobs that continue to be filled by less-educated workers, there is some evidence that employers currently seek a higher level of cognitive skills (such as reading and writing abilities, and computer skills) than they traditionally have, as well as the social skills needed to interact with customers and/or coworkers. These changes presumably reflect a variety of new developments in the workplace, among them the growing role of technology (especially computers) in many settings, changes in the organization of

[1] The deterioration in relative earnings and/or employment is documented in earlier work by Freeman and Holzer (1986) and more recently in Bound and Freeman (1992). For earlier evidence on the role of educational improvements in raising black relative wages, see Smith and Welch (1989). Evidence of the effects of federal antidiscrimination efforts appears in Heckman and Payner (1989) and Leonard (1990).

[2] The empirical literature on declining earnings for less-educated workers and on growing inequality more generally is reviewed by Levy and Murnane (1992). Other factors contributing to the decline in earnings for less-educated workers are changes in the relative supplies of college versus high school graduates, declining rates of unionism, and declining real minimum wage levels. For more specific evidence on the effects of technological change on the demand for production workers in manufacturing, see Berman, Bound, and Griliches (1994), and for evidence on the effect of computers on labor demand, see Krueger (1993). The effects of international trade on earnings and employment are evaluated by Freeman and Katz (1988), Revenga (1992), Lawrence and Slaughter (1993), and Sachs and Shatz (1994).

workplaces, and the growing competitiveness of product markets. Since the level of education and skills is generally lower among inner-city minorities than among inner-city whites, minority workers are particularly hard hit by such labor market changes.

2) *Deindustrialization.* The decline in jobs for less-educated workers has been particularly striking in the area of blue-collar employment, especially in the manufacturing sector. Manufacturing jobs are giving way to jobs in the trade and service sectors. The decline in manufacturing employment has been especially severe in the Northeast and the Midwest, and its impact has been greater among black males than among any other ethnic group. Since manufacturing jobs have traditionally paid relatively higher wages to less-educated workers than other types of jobs, these sectoral shifts appear to have significantly reduced the earnings and employment of less-educated workers, particularly of black males.

3) *Spatial Relocations of Employers.* Firms have been moving from central-city to suburban locations for several decades. This has resulted in a decline in employment opportunities for those minorities who are concentrated in inner-city areas (due to racial and/or economic segregation), and whose ability to find work in and commute to suburban areas is limited by transportation difficulties and lack of information.

4) *Racial Discrimination.* While overall discrimination in the labor market appears to have declined since the 1960s, employer fears of less-educated young black males may have risen along with the growth of inner-city crime rates. Weakened enforcement of "affirmative action" programs at the federal level may also have contributed to a rise in labor market discrimination since the 1980s.[3]

[3] The evidence of shifts in labor demand away from black employees is reviewed in Moss and Tilly (1991). The effects of declining manufacturing employment on black males can be found in Bound and Holzer (1993, 1995) and Johnson and Oliver (1992). Evidence of the growing importance of cognitive skills in the labor market can be found in Murnane, Willett, and Levy (1995); quantitative evidence of their effects on the wages and/or employment of blacks can be found in Ferguson (1993), Neal and Johnson (1994), O'Neill (1990), and Rivera-Batiz (1992), while more qualitative evidence appears in Moss and Tilly (1993). The evidence of spatial problems for blacks is summarized in Holzer (1991) and Kain (1992). For evidence of discriminatory employer attitudes against blacks, see Kirschenman and Neckerman (1991) and Fix and Struyk (1993); the former use interviews with employers, while the latter use audit studies based on matched pairs of black and white job applicants to infer these effects. Leonard

All of these hypotheses refer to major changes that appear to have occurred on the *demand* side of the labor market—that is, in the locations and characteristics of employers and jobs. These changes also imply the growth of "mismatches" between the needs of employers on the demand side of the labor market and the characteristics and attitudes of workers on the supply side of the market, especially among minorities.[4]

The mismatches may occur in skills, location, attitudes, and so forth; but they all involve an inability or unwillingness on the part of workers to adjust to the needs of employers who are currently hiring. These mismatches result in low employment rates for minority and/or less-educated workers, as well as low wages for those who do manage to find and accept some employment.[5]

But, somewhat surprisingly, almost all of the evidence to date on these shifts in labor *demand* away from less-educated and minority workers is based on data from the *supply* side of the labor market. Most studies have been based on microlevel data on the earnings and employment of individual workers from such standard sources as the Current Population Survey or the Public Use Micro Samples of the decennial census.

Shifts in labor demand have been inferred from a number of sources in such data. For instance, we have observed declines in both wages and employment for most less-educated groups, which imply shifting labor demand rather than supply. The large effects on earnings of declining manufacturing and/or blue-collar employment, both of which seem to be associated with international trade or technological changes in the workplace, also suggest the importance of shifts on the demand side of the labor market. Census data on the locations of employment and travel

---

(1990) documents the declining federal enforcement of "affirmative action" programs in the 1980s.

[4]Skill and spatial "mismatch" problems for inner-city workers have recently been emphasized by Wilson (1987) and Kasarda (1995), while this notion has been criticized by Mead (1992). For other reviews of this literature, see Holzer and Vroman (1992) and Holzer (1993).

[5]In a labor market context, "mismatch" can result in low wages on available jobs, as a relatively large supply of low-skill or inner-city labor relative to demand depresses wages. If equilibrium wages in the market fall below the minimum wage, or if workers' reservation wages exceed the wages on available jobs, such mismatch will result in low employment levels as well. For evidence on the reservation wages of young black and white workers, see Holzer (1986).

times to work by geographic area, or import penetration rates and research and development (R&D) expenditures by industry, have led to similar conclusions on the importance of demand shifts.[6]

But a great deal remains unknown about the labor demand shifts that have occurred and their effects on market outcomes. In virtually all of the work noted above, "residual" changes in employment and earnings for less-educated workers (the part not accounted for by measured factors) remain quite large, as are "within-group" and "within-sector" changes in employment and earnings (the parts not accounted for by changes in the sectoral or demographic composition of the workforce).

Thus, our understanding of these phenomena remains limited, as is our ability to devise appropriate policy responses. Indeed, even at a simple descriptive level we often lack good evidence on such demand-side characteristics as job availability and locations, and employer skill requirements and perceptions.[7] Without such information, it is difficult to design job-placement and education/training programs, which require some knowledge of what kinds of jobs are available and where they are to be found, or job-creation policies, which should be based on the overall availability of work for those with the least skills.

What we really need is a clearer picture of the demand side of the new labor market that minorities and less-educated workers face. More specifically, we need direct evidence from employers on the following issues: exactly what kinds of jobs are now being filled; where these jobs are located within metropolitan areas; what skills employers need; and how employers recruit workers and screen applicants.

In addition, we need clearer data on exactly what kinds of

[6]The correlations between wage and employment changes are emphasized in Katz and Murphy (1992); occupation and/or industry shifts are emphasized in much of this literature (see Levy and Murnane 1992). Locational data and travel times are used by Ihlanfeldt and Sjoquist (1991); import penetration rates are used by Freeman and Katz (1988) and by Revenga (1992) while R&D expenditures and other measures of technical change appear in Berman, Bound, and Griliches (see chap. 1, note 1).

[7]Exceptions to this include the report of the Secretary's Commission on Achieving Necessary Skills (SCANS), U.S. Department of Labor, as described in Packer and Wirt (1992). Survey data that are at least somewhat similar to those presented have recently been compiled for New York City by the city's Department of Employment (1994) and for Milwaukee by the Employment and Training Institute of the University of Wisconsin-Milwaukee (1994). See also Bailey's (1990) more qualitative studies of changing skill requirements in particular sectors of the economy.

workers (by race/ethnic group, gender, education level, and so forth) get hired into specific kinds of jobs, and how location, skill requirements, and employer behavior influence the observed "matches" between jobs and workers.

Such information would give us a firmer basis for judging the hypotheses that have been advanced regarding demand shifts and the employment and earnings of less-educated or minority workers. Furthermore, it would greatly enhance our ability to aim our policy responses at those sectors and locations where jobs are available and at specific barriers in the hiring process that less-advantaged groups face.

THE MULTI-CITY EMPLOYER SURVEY

In response to this need for more data on employers and jobs, I recently administered a survey to employers in four major metropolitan areas: Atlanta, Boston, Detroit, and Los Angeles. The survey is part of the broader Multi-City Study of Urban Inequality, which includes new surveys of households as well as employers, with the former focusing on racial attitudes as well as housing and labor market behavior.[8] The survey of employers included in-person, qualitative interviews with a smaller sample of employers in each city, as well as my own telephone survey of a larger sample of employers.

We carried out roughly 800 interviews with employers in each of the four major metropolitan areas from the spring of 1992 through the spring of 1994.[9] In order to coordinate our surveying with the household surveys for each city, all of the interviews in Detroit were done first—from May 1992 through early March 1993. Interviews in the other three cities began shortly afterward (in March 1993) and were completed in May 1994. The survey thus began in Detroit in roughly the trough of the last recession

[8] These surveys were administered to stratified random samples that oversampled minority households and/or those in low-income census tracts. Sample sizes varied across the four metro areas and ranged from 1,600 to 4,000. Respondents included any adult in the household above the age of twenty-one.

[9] In addition to the 800 interviews completed in each of the four major metropolitan areas, some 200 were also conducted for the city of Memphis as an extra comparison site. But given the differences between Memphis and the others in size, central-city/suburban composition, and the like, we focus exclusively on the four major metropolitan areas in this volume.

(in terms of national unemployment rates) and proceeded in all four areas through the recovery that followed.

THE FOUR CITIES

The four metropolitan areas in which the surveys were administered were chosen to generate comparisons across several dimensions.[10] Thus, we chose two metropolitan areas from the North (Boston and Detroit) as well as two from the South and/or West (Atlanta and Los Angeles). Two have large populations of blacks (Atlanta and Detroit), while two are more heterogeneous in ethnic composition (Boston and Los Angeles).

The ethnic diversity of Los Angeles relative to the other areas is illustrated in table 1.1. Minorities constitute about 60 percent of the population of Los Angeles, with Hispanics alone accounting for almost 40 percent. In Atlanta and Detroit, the minority populations are overwhelmingly black, while in Boston they are more mixed, but relatively small, parts of the total population.

Los Angeles is clearly the largest area in terms of both geography and population, and its central city dwarfs the others on both counts.[11] However, the ethnic composition of its central city does not differ substantially from that of the overall metropolitan area, perhaps because of the relatively sprawling and suburban nature of the city.[12] In comparison, the central city of Boston is quite small in area and relatively small in population.

Comparing percentages of the black residential populations in the overall metropolitan areas and in the central cities, we find

[10] The geographic areas from which employers were sampled are not the exact metropolitan statistical area (MSA) borders but generally correspond to the areas in which the household surveys were administered. These, in turn, were chosen based on judgments of what constitutes the housing and labor markets for most white and minority residents in each. For Atlanta, the sampled area for employers represents the 16 counties that currently constitute the Atlanta MSA; for Boston, the area is the Massachusetts portion of the New England Consolidated Metropolitan Area, which also includes four smaller MSAs in close proximity to Boston; for Detroit, it is the Wayne, Oakland, and Macomb tri-county area; and for Los Angeles it is Los Angeles County.

[11] Here we define "central city" as the city of Atlanta or the city of Boston. In subsequent chapters we will distinguish between these (which will be designated as "primary central cities") and other central cities in each metropolitan area.

[12] In these tabulations by the Census Bureau, relatively suburban areas, such as the San Fernando Valley, are included in the city of Los Angeles. This will not be the case when we analyze the employer data.

Table 1.1 / Metropolitan Area and Central-City Characteristics

	Atlanta	Boston	Detroit	Los Angeles
Metropolitan Area				
Square Miles	5,122	2,316	1,966	4,060
Population (thousands)	2,834	3,748	3,913	8,863
% Black	26.0	6.2	24.0	11.2
% Hispanic	2.0	5.0	1.9	37.8
% Asian	1.8	3.1	1.4	10.8
% College Graduates				
Total Population	26.8	31.1	18.4	22.3
Whites	29.2	31.8	20.2	25.6
Blacks	19.6	17.4	9.8	14.8
Unemployment Rate				
Total Labor Force	5.1	6.5	9.0	7.4
Whites	3.6	5.9	6.0	5.9
Blacks	9.6	12.6	20.6	12.0
% Live in Central City				
Total Population	13.9	15.3	26.3	39.3
Whites	7.8	11.0	7.7	36.6
Blacks	38.5	63.1	83.2	49.1
Central City				
Square Miles	132	48.4	138.7	469
Population	394	574	1,028	3,485
% Black	67.1	28.0	75.7	13.9
% Hispanic	1.8	10.8	2.8	39.9
% Asian	0.9	5.3	0.8	9.8
% College Graduates				
Total Population	26.7	30.0	9.6	23.0
Whites	51.9	36.7	12.1	28.8
Blacks	11.0	14.0	8.4	13.3
Unemployment Rate				
Total Labor Force	9.2	6.8	19.7	8.4
Whites	3.7	6.4	11.8	6.6
Blacks	12.7	13.5	22.2	13.5

NOTE: All data are from published volumes based on the 1990 Census of Population. "Metropolitan areas" are as defined in note 10 of this chapter. "Central cities" here include only the cities of Atlanta, Boston, Detroit, and Los Angeles.

that blacks are relatively concentrated in the central cities of each area. But while half or more of the black populations in the Boston and Los Angeles areas live in the central cities, they constitute well under half of the *central-city* populations in these areas.

In contrast, the residents of the central cities in both Detroit and Atlanta are predominantly black. But an important difference emerges between the two: a majority of blacks in the Atlanta metropolitan area actually live outside of the city of Atlanta, as do an even larger fraction of whites; but the vast majority of blacks in the Detroit metropolitan area live in the city, while most whites live outside it. Detroit thus appears to be by far the most racially segregated metropolitan area of the four considered here, though segregation exists to some extent in all four.[13]

Interestingly, we find that the fractions of the overall populations with college degrees are fairly comparable between the central cities and the overall metropolitan areas. But by race, white central-city residents are generally *more* likely to be college graduates than are white suburbanites, while black central-city residents are *less* likely to be college graduates than are black suburbanites. This implies somewhat different sets of residential choices for the two groups: relatively more-educated whites can find and afford attractive residences in the central cities, while for relatively more-educated blacks the suburbs remain their most attractive choices. Only in Detroit are both whites and blacks in the central city relatively less educated.

Unemployment rates for blacks in 1990 were at least twice as high as for whites in all of the metropolitan areas, but for blacks in Detroit unemployment was especially severe. Whites as well as blacks residing in each central city had higher unemployment rates than those residing outside the city, but only in Detroit do central-city whites look significantly worse off than their suburban counterparts. These numbers also imply relatively low unemployment rates for blacks living outside the central city in Atlanta.[14]

[13]Detroit appears to be the most segregated of any large metropolitan area in the United States as of 1990 (Frey and Farley 1993). The Atlanta metropolitan area is also more segregated than these numbers suggest, since most blacks there live in the "southern" suburbs, while most whites live in the "northern" suburbs (Ihlanfeldt 1994).

[14]The implied unemployment rate among black suburbanites is 7.5 percent, while the comparable numbers are above 10 percent in all other areas.

Figure 1.1 / Monthly Unemployment Rates by Metropolitan Area

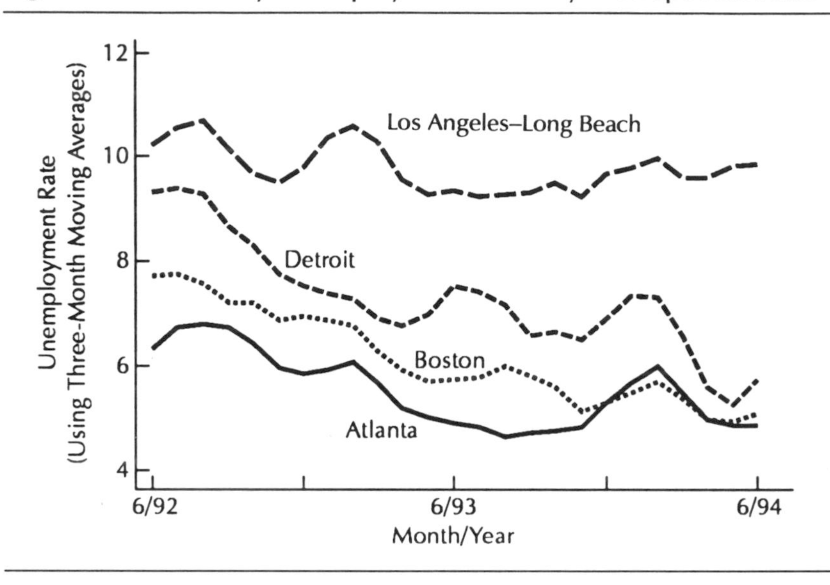

NOTE: These data appear in *Employment and Earnings* from U.S. Department of Labor.

Since the surveys were administered to firms in the period between 1992 and 1994, during which time the national economy was recovering from recession, we also plotted the monthly unemployment rates for these metropolitan areas during this period.[15] The plots show declining unemployment within each area (see figure 1.1), though the declines are smaller in Los Angeles than elsewhere. The lowest overall rates occurred in Atlanta, which appears to be enjoying a pre-1996 Olympics boom. Detroit and Los Angeles had the highest rates during the survey periods.[16] Los Angeles was apparently suffering through a post-1980s slump, as well as from the likely negative labor market effects of the racial disturbances of April 1992 and the Northridge earthquake in 1994.

[15] We present three-month moving averages of monthly rates to eliminate some of the random fluctuations in the latter.

[16] While unemployment rates in Detroit recovered quite dramatically between 1992 and 1994, most of the surveying there actually occurred during 1992, when rates were quite high.

In sum, we looked at four cities with a wide range of economic, geographic, and demographic characteristics. The starkest contrasts between whites and blacks, and also between the central city and the suburbs, are found in Detroit and, to a lesser degree, in Atlanta, though black suburbanites are found in the latter in more substantial numbers than in the other metropolitan areas and are doing well by at least some measures. In contrast, in the smaller city of Boston and the larger city of Los Angeles major black/white gaps in employment also can be found, but amid more diverse ethnic environments and with less striking contrasts between the suburbs and the central cities.

In comparing the percentages of all employed people who live in the central cities versus the percentages of those who work there (see table 1.2), we find that there is net commuting of workers from outlying areas into the central cities in all of these metropolitan areas. The amounts of in-commuting for Atlanta and Boston look particularly substantial.

We also calculated the percentages of the residents in each location (in the central city or elsewhere) who work in the central cities as well as the percentages of workers in each central city

Table 1.2 / Work/Residence Locations and Travel Patterns

	Atlanta	Boston	Detroit	Los Angeles
% of Employed Who Live in Central City	10.4	15.1	19.1	39.6
% Who Work in the Central City Among				
All Employed	26.6	24.4	20.5	41.6
Central-City Residents	67.3	69.2	56.2	68.8
Other Residents	20.6	16.6	12.2	23.8
% of Employees in the Central City Who Are				
Central-City Residents	30.1	42.0	51.8	65.5
Other Residents	69.9	58.0	48.2	24.5
% Who Drive to Work				
Total Population	90.7	79.0	93.3	85.6
Whites	94.0	82.9	95.3	87.6
Blacks	81.2	58.5	84.1	85.2

who reside in either location. These numbers show that roughly two-thirds of the central-city residents of most metropolitan areas work in the central cities (except in Detroit, where the percentage is somewhat lower), whereas much smaller percentages of non-central-city residents (12–24 percent) work in the central cities. Thus, place of residence clearly matters a great deal in terms of where people work (and likely the reverse is also true).

Given the far larger residential populations of the non-central-city areas, however, the commuters from these areas add very significantly to the supplies of labor inside the central cities. Indeed, in Atlanta and Boston the commuters constitute significant majorities of central-city employees.

Taken together, these data generally imply *higher ratios of jobs to people in the central cities* than in the other parts of the metropolitan areas—despite the growing suburbanization of jobs over time that has been documented elsewhere (Kasarda 1995). Detroit is again an exception, with more jobs per person in the suburbs than in the central city.[17]

But, while many jobs exist in the central cities, local residents do not always get them. Indeed, the central cities remain net importers of workers: more people commute from the suburbs to central cities for work than engage in "reverse commuting" from the city to the suburbs. This appears to be somewhat less true for blacks than for whites, since the former are so much more likely to live in the central city in the first place.[18] (The implications of both job location and commuting behavior for the number of jobs available to central-city residents will be considered in the next chapter.)

Finally, we note that almost comparable fractions of white and black workers in Los Angeles drive to work, while in the other areas significantly fewer blacks do so than whites. Automobile transit appears to be less heavily used in Boston than elsewhere,

[17] While there are more workers in the central city of Detroit than there are *employed* residents there, there are fewer workers than residents there. Thus, in table 1.1 we see that 26 percent of all metropolitan area residents live in the central city, but in table 1.2 we find that just 20 percent of the employed work there.

[18] The data on place of work by specific city were not available in the published Census volumes by race. However, data on central cities versus suburbs more generally show that the ratios of jobs to residences in the central cities are higher for whites than for blacks.

especially in the central city (where most blacks reside); this may well reflect Boston's relatively smaller city size and/or the higher quality of mass transit there.

SURVEY QUESTIONS AND SAMPLING ISSUES

The questions in our survey dealt with a variety of firm-level and job-specific hiring topics. These included gross and net hiring during the previous year; the number and characteristics of vacant jobs; an extensive set of questions on the last worker hired and job filled, including task performance, recruitment and screening procedures, wages and benefits, demographics of the new employee, and promotions or turnover since the date of hiring; and various other characteristics of the firm (industry, unionism, recent sales growth, for example) and its overall workforce. The survey respondent was the person identified as being responsible for new hiring (usually for positions not requiring college degrees) in the firm.

The samples of firms were drawn from two sources: the current or most recent employer reported by respondents in the corresponding household survey (from the multi-city study) for each city, and listings of employers in each area drawn primarily (though not exclusively) from telephone directories and provided by Survey Sampling Inc. (SSI).

The specifications were somewhat different for each of these two samples. The SSI sample was restricted to employers who had hired an employee for a position that did not require a college graduate within the previous three years. For the household-based sample, employers had to have hired an employee in the past three years into the same occupation that was held by the household respondent who generated the employer name (though the source was not divulged to employers in either case). Thus, employers who had recently hired college graduates could appear in either part of the sample, though jobs *requiring* college graduates should only have appeared in the household-based sample.

Unfortunately, the number of firms linked to households in each city varied according to the timing of the household surveys. Since the Boston and Los Angeles household surveys were the

Table 1.3 / Sample Sizes Generated By Two Sources

	Household Generated	SSI Generated
Atlanta	296	517
Boston	160	639
Detroit	425	380
Los Angeles	125	678
Totals	1,006	2,214

last to be administered, and since their completion dates ranged well beyond the completion date for the employer survey, the numbers of employers generated by households were limited in these cities, as can be seen in table 1.3.[19]

The number of household-generated employers in Detroit was especially high, since we also sampled from a youth follow-up survey there (which generated 120 such employers) that was not conducted in the other cities.[20]

In addition to providing us with linked employer-household pairs, samples of firms generated by households are more likely to contain the kinds of very new and/or small firms that may be missed when relying on telephone directories. On the other hand, variation in the willingness or ability of household respondents to divulge a correct employer name and address may have limited the representativeness of that part of the sample, especially if there are systematic differences across demographic groups (such as by educational attainment or race) in such behavior. The "informal sector" of the economy is likely to be underreported in the data from both sources, though this is certainly also true of employer data from other sources (such as the data compiled by the Bureau of Labor Statistics).

[19] The surveying of households in Boston and Los Angeles did not get under way until the summer of 1993 and was not completed until late 1994. The greater ethnic diversity of the respondents in these areas, the need to translate the survey into Spanish and Chinese, and the general need to match ethnicities between households and interviewers all contributed to the delays experienced in these metropolitan areas. Since the employer survey was completed by the spring of 1994, there was only a limited period of overlap in which employers generated by these households could be screened and interviewed.

[20] An additional 600 firms that are matched to households in Los Angeles and Boston were later surveyed by some colleagues in the MCSUI project, but these were not included in the sample analyzed here.

The samples of firms from both sources should approximate *employee-weighted* samples of firms in each metropolitan area—in other words, samples where firms are represented in proportion to the numbers of workers they employ. The household-generated firms will do so only after they are sample-weighted, using weights from the household survey that help us reproduce a random sample of employees in each area.[21]

The SSI sample was stratified when drawn on the basis of employer size, with extra weight put on larger firms so as to approximate the distribution of firm sizes among the workforce.[22] Thus, no weights were necessary here to generate an employee-weighted sample for this part of the survey.[23] But additional sample weights were calculated to correct for the underrepresentation of workers hired into college-graduate positions in the SSI sample and for any nonrandomness in the Boston and Los Angeles samples caused by timing discrepancies between the employer and household surveys.[24]

Even with the use of sampling weights, it is possible that non-

[21] These sample weights, computed in each case by the firms that implemented the survey, adjust for the probabilities of household selection (the overrepresentation of households in predominantly minority or low-income census tracts), numbers of eligible respondents in the households, and nonresponse rates for some different categories of respondents. The sample weights should therefore generate a random sample of adults within the metropolitan area, and their employers should represent an employee-weighted sample of firms.

[22] The firms were sampled as follows: 25 percent from firms with 1–19 employees; 50 percent from firms with 20–99 employees; and 25 percent from firms with 100 or more employees. This distribution approximates the one found among firms in the Employment Opportunity Pilot Project (EOPP) sample of firms from 1980 and 1982.

[23] Ex-ante measures of firm (or establishment) size were developed by SSI. These were done primarily on the basis of very detailed industry-by-area averages, though the numbers were actually confirmed through telephone calls in at least some cases. Of course, given the well-known instability of employment at the establishment level (Davis and Haltiwanger 1990), it is inevitable that *ex-post* measures will differ from *ex-ante* ones, even where the latter are correct. More evidence on the distribution of firms in this study by size category appears in chapter 2.

[24] The weights on those working in positions requiring college degrees adjusts for the fact that only the firms generated from household surveys were supposed to generate workers in non-college positions. Thus, to generate an accurate sample of these workers, the weight used is essentially the ratio of total firms to household-generated firms in each city (with a correction for SSI firms in each city that mistakenly provided such a position). The additional weights for Los Angeles and Boston adjust for any over- or underrepresentation of firms from black, Hispanic, and/or Asian household respondents, since only some relatively early subsamples from these groups of firms were actually included in the sample.

randomness might have been introduced by systematic variation in the rates at which truly eligible firms were successfully screened or in the rates at which screened firms actually completed interviews. Such variation might be a source of *selection bias* in any estimated statistics if selection into the sample varies systematically in ways that might affect our analysis.[25]

Fortunately, we have some data on three characteristics of SSI firms (regarding location, type of industry, and size) that did not make it through the screening process or did not respond to the survey. Comparisons between these firms and the survey respondents enabled us to test for such systematic differences across firms in screening and response rates, at least along these three observable dimensions.

An analysis of response rates by these categories may be found in appendix A. These show few large or statistically significant differences in response rates that would generate such bias. Our overall response rate of roughly 67 percent among screened firms also compares favorably with other large-scale telephone surveys that have recently been implemented.[26]

In the chapters that follow, we present evidence from this survey on employers, jobs, and newly hired workers in the four metropolitan areas. We focus particularly on jobs that do not require college degrees and workers who do not have them, and also on employment outcomes for minorities and women relative to those of white males.

We present mostly summary data on jobs and workers hired, frequently cross-tabulated by metropolitan area, by locations within these areas (central city versus suburb), and by occupations or industry. These data are primarily descriptive, though they generate some striking findings that often suggest certain causal interpretations.

The latter are also tested more formally with some multivariate regression analyses of employment and wages for various demo-

[25]The classic analysis of sample selection bias appears in Heckman (1979).

[26]Recent employer surveys, both by mail and phone, are reviewed in a report on workplace innovations prepared by the U.S. Department of Labor (1993). Another large sample survey that was designed as a followup to the EOPP study recently achieved a response rate of 51 percent (see Barron, Berger, and Black 1994).

graphic groups. These appear toward the ends of chapters 4 and 5. For readers who are not entirely comfortable with this level of statistical analysis, these sections can be skipped over without any great loss of content.

In chapter 2, we examine the overall characteristics of firms and jobs that have been filled recently. These characteristics include wages and benefits provided, occupations and types of industries, establishment size, and the location of firms within the metropolitan area. Location is particularly important because it sheds light on the spatial issues alluded to. Some data on hiring, turnover, and job vacancy rates are also provided as additional evidence on the overall numbers of available jobs for less-educated workers.

In chapter 3, we consider the skill requirements of employers, as defined by the tasks that must be performed in the newly filled jobs. We also look at the recruitment and screening methods used by employers to fill these jobs, and at some data on employer willingness to hire from different groups of workers. The relatively high level of tasks required for jobs usually considered low wage or low skill, especially relative to the limited skills and credentials that many workers bring to the labor market, are highlighted. We also discuss the implications of these findings for the current debate on "welfare reform." Most proposals for reform implicitly assume that sufficient numbers of low-skill jobs will be available to employ all welfare mothers who enter the labor market; our findings cast some doubt on that assumption.

In chapter 4, we look at who actually gets hired into various kinds of jobs. Our main focus is on the determinants of hiring by race and gender, specifically on how the task needs and the screening processes used by employers are related to the likelihood that black males or black females are hired for these positions. We also compare data on hiring with respect to black male, black female, and Hispanic applicants. By controlling for differences in applicant rates from different groups, we get cleaner measures of relative *demand* by employers for applicants of the different groups and a better idea of how this varies by location and type of job. The differences in applicant rates to firms across locations, occupations, and industries also give us insights into spatial problems and other factors that affect the *supply* of black or Hispanic labor to various types of firms. The chapter concludes with some logistical (or logit) regression analysis of the determinants of hiring for specific race and gender groups.

In chapter 5, we examine evidence of the wages earned by different groups of workers, beginning with tabular evidence on wage differences across race/gender groups, overall, and by educational group and industry. We then use regression analysis to estimate the fractions of the observed wage differences across groups that might be attributable to discrimination, as opposed to those accounted for by observable differences in worker skills and job requirements.

In chapter 6, we summarize our findings and present our conclusions, along with what we see as the policy implications of our findings and directions for further study.

PRINCIPAL FINDINGS

Before moving on, it may be useful to enumerate our principal findings:

- There are fewer vacant jobs available to unemployed workers who live in the central cities than in the suburbs, yet the vacancies in the central cities often take as long or longer to fill;
- Most of the jobs available to less-educated workers, especially in the central cities, are in white-collar or service occupations in the retail trade and service sectors;
- Almost all of the jobs in both locations require daily reading/writing and arithmetic tasks, computer use, and/or customer contact;
- Many jobs are filled through informal recruitment channels, especially through current employees;
- Almost all employers require certain credentials from applicants, such as high school diplomas, job-specific experience, references, and/or previous vocational training before hiring;
- Employers seem wary of workers with unstable work histories, especially of those with criminal records (whether actual or suspected);
- Even for non-college jobs, task requirements and hiring screens for jobs located in the central cities are somewhat higher than those in the suburbs;
- The hiring of minorities for many jobs, even those that do not require college degrees, appears to be limited by the skill require-

ments of those jobs relative to the skill levels that employers perceive among these applicants;

- Black applicants, particularly black males, appear to be additionally disadvantaged in gaining employment as a result of where they live (they tend to apply for jobs in the central cities, while many more low-skill jobs are available in the suburbs) and by employer discrimination in hiring;
- Low starting wages and benefits characterize many non-college jobs, especially for minorities and females; and
- *Wage* discrimination still appears to limit the earnings of women relative to those of men (despite some relative progress made during the past decade).

Overall, we find a labor market in which *skills, the locations of firms and workers,* and *race and gender* all play critical roles in determining who gets hired and what workers are paid. The employment and earnings prospects of less-educated and less-skilled workers, especially among minorities and those with limited work experience (such as long-term welfare recipients), look particularly grim.

If the government enacts welfare reform and other legislation that is built on the expectation (or embodies the requirement) that all able-bodied adults will be able to find jobs, we will need to develop policies that address the specific barriers that the less-educated face in today's labor market. A greater understanding of these barriers is what we hope to develop below.

2 / What Jobs Are There and Where Are They?

In conducting our survey of employers to gather data on the numbers of new jobs that are available, we were particularly interested in the question of where these jobs are located—not only geographically but also in which industries, with what size employers, and whether they are in firms with collective-bargaining agreements. Therefore we begin by presenting some general descriptive material on these characteristics for the firms in our sample. Because the sample of employers is employee-weighted, these characteristics also reflect the characteristics of the jobs currently held by the overall workforce.[1]

But this raises the question of exactly how we should measure the number of jobs that are currently available in these firms to people seeking work. A variety of measures appear in our survey that capture some dimension of new job availability at the firm level, such as the total number of new hires (or *gross* hires) in the previous year; the number of *net* hires, after adjusting for turnover; and the number of job *vacancies* at the time of the survey.

While each of these measures tells us something about new job availability in the labor markets of the cities we surveyed, each

[1] Until we consider the characteristics of recently filled jobs or hired workers later in this work, we will focus on *all* firms (not only those hiring into non-college positions).

also has its limitations. Therefore we also look at some of the characteristics of the most recently filled job in each firm, such as occupation, starting wages, and benefits. Since our sample is essentially an employee-weighted sample of firms, we argue that this sample of jobs roughly approximates the one that workers face when seeking new employment in the labor market.

In the following chapters we will focus on this sample of jobs and consider in more detail their skill requirements, the hiring activity of employers, the workers hired into these jobs, and the wages they receive. When discussing these job or worker characteristics, we will usually limit the sample to those positions that do *not* require a four-year college degree.

CHARACTERISTICS OF FIRMS

Table 2.1 presents data on the distributions of the firms surveyed across locations within the metropolitan areas and across industries and data on the existence of collective-bargaining agreements

Table 2.1 / Characteristics of Firms

	Atlanta	Boston	Detroit	Los Angeles
Location				
Primary Central City	.437	.168	.167	.261
Suburb	.360	.630	.679	.630
Other	.203	.202	.154	.109
Industry				
Construction	.025	.017	.030	.014
Manufacturing	.185	.234	.166	.245
Transportation, Communications, and Utilities	.062	.060	.056	.050
Wholesale Trade	.106	.044	.070	.066
Retail Trade	.173	.144	.213	.147
Finance, Insurance, and Real Estate	.079	.099	.095	.081
Services	.356	.393	.344	.397
Public	.014	.009	.026	.010
Collective Bargaining	.074	.167	.216	.190

NOTE: Columns under each metropolitan area for "Location" and "Industry" each sum approximately to one, with any discrepancies (in this and subsequent tables) caused by rounding error or missing values.

for each of the four metropolitan areas in our study. Industries are defined broadly (at the 1-digit level according to Standard Industrial Classification code), and collective bargaining is measured by the percentage of employees who are covered at the establishment level.

Location within the metropolitan area is measured by whether a firm is found in the primary central city, the suburbs, or in "other" parts of the metropolitan areas.[2] The primary central cities are the cities of Atlanta, Boston, Detroit, and Los Angeles, whereas the "other" areas include other central cities in each of the four metropolitan areas in addition to the primary ones (as designated by the Census Bureau), as well as all other municipalities whose residents are at least 30 percent black.[3]

Although the "central city/suburb" distinction is a crude tool for analyzing issues based on location within metropolitan areas (because of the heterogeneity of neighborhoods or municipalities *within* these categories), it is a reasonable geographic "first cut" that can be applied consistently to all four areas under discussion.[4] Furthermore, the distinction between "suburbs" and "other" areas enables us to distinguish between areas outside the primary central city that are more rather than less commercial and more rather than less populated by monitories.

The data show that, in three of the four metropolitan areas, roughly two-thirds of jobs are located in the suburbs; about a sixth

[2] Locations of firms within metropolitan areas are based on the cities that are listed in their mailing addresses. For most locations, this seems to generate a fairly reasonable approximation to the boundaries of central cities and suburban areas, with a few exceptions that are described below.

[3] The Census Bureau defines each of the following municipalities as a central city: (1) the largest (by population) within each metropolitan area; (2) any having at least 250,000 residents; (3) any having at least 25,000 residents in which the ratio of employees to residents is at least .75 and in which at least 40 percent of the workers who live in the city also work there; and (4) any having at least 15,000 residents and that is at least a third the size of the largest central city and meets the last two criteria under (3). In the Atlanta MSA, Marietta is defined as a central city; in the Boston Consolidated Metropolitan Area, these include Brockton, Cambridge, Framingham, Gloucester, Haverhill, Lawrence, Lowell, Lynn, Salem, and Waltham; in Detroit, they include Pontiac and Dearborn; and in Los Angeles, they include Long Beach, Pasadena, and Pomona. The fractions of populations in each municipality that are black were obtained from the 1990 Census of Population, and are available from the author.

[4] This heterogeneity argues for other analyses at more detailed geographic levels (such as the census tract) that are currently under way.

to a quarter are located in the primary central cities; and the rest (10–20 percent) are found in the "other" areas.

These results roughly parallel those derived from the census data on workplace locations presented in chapter 1, though there are a few discrepancies that seem to reflect differences in the drawing of city boundaries or in our response rates across locations.[5] But the finding that there are more jobs than people in the primary central cities except for Detroit seems to hold up when these numbers are compared to the population estimates of table 1.1.[6]

Furthermore, if we perform separate computations for jobs requiring college degrees and those that do not, we find that net in-commuting to jobs located in the primary central cities occurs among both the educated and less-educated populations in these metropolitan areas.[7]

By industry, we find that 60–65 percent of jobs are in retail trade, the financial sector, or the service sector in each metropolitan area, with manufacturing accounting for just 16–25 percent. These numbers are broadly consistent with those observed in the Bureau of Labor Statistics' *County Business Patterns* data for these same metropolitan areas, which confirms the general representativeness of our sample of employers.[8] We also find that only 7–22 percent of jobs are covered by collective-bargaining

[5]The fraction of jobs that we find in central-city Atlanta seems to overestimate the actual number, probably because the use of mailing addresses there attributes some suburban locations to the central city. This could possibly lead to some downward biases in our estimates of differences between the two types of areas. In Los Angeles, our estimate is considerably lower than that of the census, since we do not count areas such as the San Fernando valley as part of the primary central city (while the census does). In Boston and Detroit, our estimates of jobs in the central cities are also a bit lower, perhaps due to the lower response rates we achieved among central-city firms relative to other firms.

[6]Again, our estimate for Los Angeles does not replicate what we found in chapter 1, since the central-city populations from the census include the areas that we excluded from our sample of central-city firms.

[7]Specifically, the roughly one-fourth of new jobs that require college degrees in these firms are evenly split between central cities and suburbs, as are the college and non-college populations in these areas (from table 1.1). However, since there are relatively more white than black college graduates residing in the central cities, these numbers imply relatively more in-commuting among less-educated than more educated whites.

[8]In the published data for 1991, manufacturing accounts for 13–24 percent of employment in each of the four metropolitan areas. Comparable ranges for retail trade and the non-financial services are 17–21 percent and 31–40 percent, respectively.

agreements, mirroring the decline in private-sector unionism in the United States that has been noted elsewhere.[9]

The results of our survey show that manufacturing establishments are significantly more likely to be located in the suburbs, while financial and service establishments are more likely to be found in the primary central cities. (See table 2.2.) This is true for each of the four metropolitan areas.[10] These results are broadly consistent with those of Kasarda (1995) and others who have described the movement of manufacturing employment away from central cities and their replacement with a variety of services. Indeed, this trend has been occurring for several decades and can probably be attributed to a variety of economic forces that differ across these industries.[11]

But whether this implies that central-city residents, and minorities in particular, have less access to employment in manufacturing and/or blue-collar jobs more generally depends on where they live within the metropolitan areas, and on the opportunities for or costs of commuting.

We also note that the firms in the areas designated as "other" show little consistent pattern relative to those in the primary central cities or suburbs, in terms of these characteristics. This is not surprising given that the municipalities in this category are a diverse group whose composition varies. Therefore, most of our comparisons focus on the differences between primary central-city and suburban areas.[12]

[9] See, for instance, Freeman and Medoff (1984).

[10] Most differences in means across categories discussed here and below are *statistically significant*. Standard errors on dichotomous variables can be calculated as the square root of (P * (1 − P)/N), where P is the mean and N is the sample size. Standard errors on *differences* across nonintersecting categories can be calculated as the square root of the sum of the squared individual standard errors.

[11] For instance, manufacturing requires a good deal of land, which can be more cheaply obtained in outlying areas, while the services and financial sectors often need to be close to one another and to centers of educated labor. See, for instance, Stanback and Knight (1976).

[12] In Atlanta and Detroit, the "other" areas are more likely to be predominantly black residential areas, while in Boston and Los Angeles they are mostly other central cities. This might help to account for some of the distinctions across the metropolitan areas in the characteristics of these localities. In subsequent chapters, results for the "other" areas will often lie in between those for "primary central cities" and "suburbs."

Another important characteristic with respect to employers and jobs is the average size of the establishment (in terms of numbers of employees), which can have important effects on a variety of labor market outcomes (Brown, Hamilton, and Medoff 1990). A variety of data on establishment size appear in tables B.1 and B.2 in appendix B. Since the sample is weighted by employees, these data do *not* reflect the average sizes of establishments but rather the sizes of the establishments in which we find the average employee (which will be more heavily weighted toward larger firms). Overall, these data are fairly comparable to those on the distributions of employees by size categories that appear in *County Business Patterns.*[13]

These data reveal, first, that average establishment size is largest in the services category and smallest in the retail trade category. Second, establishments are generally larger in the primary central cities than in other areas, but this is primarily true for services and *not* in manufacturing and retail trade.[14] And, third, "temporary" and/or "contracted" employees currently account for about 5–10 percent of all employees, and presumably larger fractions among new hires, with the highest concentrations appearing in the services.

NEW HIRES, TURNOVER, AND VACANCIES

While these data describe overall employment levels in different industries and geographic locations, they tell us little about job availability for those workers who are currently seeking employment.

There are several measures here of such job availability. These include: the *gross hire rate,* which is the rate at which new workers were hired in the preceding year; the *net hire rate,* which is the rate at which employment at firms grew over this period; the *turnover rate,* which for our purposes is based on quits and dis-

[13] In the published data, roughly 44 percent of all employment is accounted for by firms with 100 or more employees; 30 percent by firms with 20–99 employees; and the rest by firms with 19 or fewer employees.

[14] The substantially larger fraction of service establishments in the 1,000+ category (relative to other industries) reflects hospitals and schools, among other types of business.

Table 2.2 / Percentage of Jobs by Industry and of Jobs Covered by Collective-Bargaining Agreements

	Atlanta			Boston		
	PCC[a]	SUB[b]	OTH[c]	PCC	SUB	OTH
Industry						
Construction	.020	.025	.038	.023	.020	.000
Manufacturing	.100	.275	.209	.092	.239	.335
Transportation, Communications, and Utilities	.085	.044	.043	.067	.072	.019
Wholesale Trade	.093	.101	.142	.015	.055	.032
Retail Trade	.162	.208	.137	.164	.157	.089
Finance, Insurance, and Real Estate	.134	.035	.037	.158	.086	.082
Services	.397	.287	.388	.459	.365	.424
Public	.009	.026	.006	.022	.005	.010
Collective Bargaining	.094	.054	.069	.122	.155	.242

[a] Primary central city.
[b] Suburbs.
[c] Other central cities or municipalities with at least 30 percent black residential populations.

charges;[15] and the *job vacancy rate,* which is the fraction of all jobs in a firm that are currently not filled.

The hiring and turnover rates are defined here as fractions of each establishment's implied employment level one year previous to the survey, while the vacancy rate is defined as a fraction of total jobs (filled or vacant) in the firm at the time of the survey. These calculated rates are based on explicit survey questions for each establishment regarding the number of new hires in the previous year, turnover in specific categories (such as quits and discharges), and the number of jobs vacant at the time of the survey.

The hiring and turnover rates represent *flows* of employees into and out of firms over a particular time period, while the vacancy rates measure *stocks* of available jobs at a given time. Gross hire

[15] We focus on the two components of turnover that are more likely to reflect steady-state employment at a firm rather than on those associated with net gains or losses of employment, such as layoffs or recalls, that should presumably be captured by measures of net hiring.

	Detroit			Los Angeles		
	PCC	SUB	OTH	PCC	SUB	OTH
Industry						
Construction	.016	.037	.014	.005	.014	.035
Manufacturing	.096	.199	.093	.199	.272	.195
Transportation, Communications, and Utilities	.029	.053	.102	.089	.036	.035
Wholesale Trade	.065	.060	.121	.077	.068	.023
Retail Trade	.146	.237	.179	.102	.176	.085
Finance, Insurance, and Real Estate	.121	.085	.114	.079	.078	.108
Services	.502	.300	.365	.448	.348	.470
Public	.027	.029	.010	.000	.008	.049
Collective Bargaining	.296	.199	.199	.207	.158	.332

rates should reflect both job turnover and recent net employment growth for firms, while overall vacancy rates should depend on the amount of gross hiring (which determines the *frequencies* of vacancies, or the number of times they occur) as well as the amount of time it takes to fill each position (or average *durations* of vacancies). Indeed, the vacancy rate (like the unemployment rate) can be broken down into its frequency and duration components, and a change in either component will comparably change the overall rate.[16]

The means for all of these measures of new job availability, as well as correlations across the various measures,[17] are shown in table B.3 in appendix B. The means indicate that roughly a fourth

[16] For a new hire to be listed as a job vacancy, the new position must not be filled instantly (i.e., the duration must be nonzero), and the firm must have formal enough employment categories to have explicit jobs that are either filled or vacant. See Mincer (1966) and Holzer (1994a) for discussion and evidence on these issues.

[17] This table, and those which follow it, presents means of rates rather than rates calculated on mean levels of hires, vacancies, and employment for each establishment. The latter would give more weight to larger establishments, but this we have accomplished through our sampling strategy, which implicitly weights by establishment size.

of all employees have been hired within the previous twelve months, though this primarily reflects turnover (especially from quits) rather than net employment growth. These findings are broadly consistent with other recent evidence of high turnover and large gross employment flows at the establishment level (see Davis and Haltiwanger 1990; Anderson and Meyer 1994).[18]

Gross hiring and quit and discharge rates are also very highly correlated across establishments, suggesting again that the former is largely driven by the latter two. The net hiring rates that are directly *reported* by firms are considerably higher than those that are *implied* by the turnover and gross hire rates,[19] but both are positive, as they should be during a period of recovery from recession.[20]

Despite the large amount of gross hiring that occurs, the mean job vacancy rate (2.7 percent) is a good deal lower than the aggregate unemployment rate (6–7 percent) for the period surveyed. This is also consistent with other evidence from various points in the business cycle (Abraham 1983; Holzer 1993; Holzer 1994a).[21]

The lower vacancy than unemployment rates seem to mostly reflect shorter *durations* for the vacancies (although the frequencies of the two measures should be more equal).[22] The lower vacancy

[18] Davis and Haltiwanger present data from the Longitudinal Research Datafile from the Bureau of Labor Statistics. These data include births and deaths of firms over time as well as net growth for existing establishments, though they are based only on data for the manufacturing sector. The data in Anderson and Meyer are from a matched file of employee wage and unemployment insurance records from eight states.

[19] The directly reported rates are from a survey question on the net change in employment over the previous year. The implied rates were based on net changes calculated as gross hires + recalls − (quits + discharges + layoffs). Both measures were then calculated as percentages of earlier employment levels.

[20] The absence here of data on births and deaths of firms makes it impossible to compare the gross and net employment growth measures directly to those of other studies or to the labor force growth for the relevant metropolitan areas.

[21] The ratio of vacancy to unemployment rates here is comparable to those calculated by Abraham for various areas and time periods during the 1970s. The ratio here is actually higher than those observed in my earlier work, since the latter was based on data from recessionary labor markets in 1980 and 1982.

[22] Each episode of job turnover should add equally to the frequencies of vacant jobs and unemployed workers; if the vacant jobs get filled more quickly than the unemployed workers are hired, unemployment rates will exceed vacancy rates. One reason for longer durations of unemployment than of vacancies might be that vacancies are always costly to employers (in terms of lost output and profits), while some periods of unemployment may not be for workers (such as when they are collecting unemployment insurance).

rates do imply that, *at any given time*, there are not sufficient numbers of jobs available for all unemployed workers who want them. In some sense, a fairly large number of unemployed workers are "queuing" for a fairly small number of available jobs, even when the overall economy is at the peak of the business cycle.[23]

But if jobs become vacant frequently enough over time, unemployment durations for most groups of workers need not be terribly long, and most should move through the "hiring queue" with reasonable speed. Indeed, median unemployment spells in *nonrecessionary* times are generally about a month in duration (Feldstein 1973; Sider 1985).[24]

On the other hand, there are specific groups in the population (for example, minorities, the young, and/or the least educated) who always experience much lengthier spells without work and who are viewed by employers as being at the "back of the queue" of potential workers in terms of expected productivity.[25] It is for these groups that a major *lack of job availability* can exist even in good times, which then worsens when the overall ratio of unemployment to vacancies is higher.

Additional data on hiring, turnover rates, and job vacancy rates are presented in tables 2.3–2.5. Mean hiring, turnover, and va-

[23] Whether or not this imbalance between unemployment and vacancy rates suggests that the aggregate labor market is not in "equilibrium" or at "full employment" depends on one's definitions of these terms. Most macroeconomists use stable inflation rates as the relevant criterion, resulting in concepts such as the "natural rate of unemployment" and the "non-accelerating inflation rate of unemployment." These criteria do not necessarily involve overall equality between unemployment and vacancy rates. But *frictional* as well as *structural* (or mismatch) unemployment can certainly exist at the "natural rate," and the structural type can entail very high unemployment rates for *specific* groups, such as those with the lowest skills. There can also be considerable variance across local areas when the aggregate economy is at the "natural rate," with some areas (Boston in the late 1980s, for example) having very tight labor markets and others containing more slack.

[24] Average unemployment *durations* are generally two to three times as long as vacancy durations (and longer in recessions). These ratios appear to account for the overall ratio of unemployment to vacancy *rates* noted above; this also implies that the *frequencies* of the two measures should be fairly comparable—that a job vacancy occurs at some point for each worker who becomes unemployed.

[25] Durations of *non*employment spells, even for those who are generally attached to the labor force, are longer than those of *un*employment, since the nonemployment spells include periods of time in which workers may temporarily stop seeking work (as defined by the Bureau of Labor Statistics). *Mean* durations can also be substantially higher than medians, due to a high concentration of very lengthy spells among groups, such as young blacks (Clark and Summers 1982; Ballen and Freeman 1986).

cancy rates by location within each metropolitan area appear in the first of these tables; ratios of unemployed workers and vacant jobs for the primary central cities relative to the metropolitan areas overall appear in the second; and data on the characteristics of the vacant jobs, such as their durations and distributions across occupations, appear in the third.[26] Data comparable to those in table 2.3 for the three largest industries are shown in table B.4 in appendix B.

Across metropolitan areas, we generally find that job vacancy rates are lowest in Los Angeles, where unemployment rates were highest at the time of the survey (see figure 1.1). Across industries, as table B.4 indicates, turnover, hiring, and vacancy rates are all generally lower in manufacturing than in retail trade and the service sector. The lower turnover likely reflects the higher relative wages that are paid in manufacturing, while the lower hiring rates appear to reflect both lower turnover and lower employment growth of manufacturing in recent years.[27]

Across locations within the metropolitan areas, as the data in table 2.3 suggest, discharge rates are comparable or higher in the primary central cities than in the suburbs or the "other" areas, perhaps indicating some greater employer dissatisfaction with the local workforce; on the other hand, quit rates in the central cities are generally lower than elsewhere.[28] Overall turnover rates thus do not appear to differ substantially between central cities and the suburbs.

Similarly, neither hiring nor vacancy rates are consistently higher or lower in the primary central-city areas. This is true despite the fact that the ratios of jobs to people are generally higher in the central cities, as we saw in chapter 1.

Comparable vacancy rates, along with higher numbers of jobs

[26] The durations are defined for the job with the longest vacancy duration that exists at any given firm, while the occupational distributions appear for all vacancies and separately for the longest ones.

[27] For evidence of higher relative wages in manufacturing, see Krueger and Summers (1987). Lower turnover rates among higher-wage employees are discussed in Parsons (1986).

[28] These findings are consistent with the higher discharge rates for minorities that have been found by Ferguson and Filer (1986). Quit rates are also higher for minorities but not after controlling for job characteristics and wages (see, for instance, Parsons 1986).

Table 2.3 / Mean Hiring, Turnover, and Vacancy Rates

	Atlanta			Boston			Detroit			Los Angeles		
	PCC[a]	SUB[b]	OTH[c]	PCC	SUB	OTH	PCC	SUB	OTH	PCC	SUB	OTH
Gross Hire Rate	.283	.276	.237	.198	.193	.228	.227	.310	.388	.230	.265	.172
Turnover Rates												
Quits	.152	.174	.174	.119	.104	.137	.124	.160	.217	.111	.145	.141
Discharges	.093	.079	.070	.062	.051	.047	.064	.047	.106	.072	.077	.067
Job Vacancy Rate	.028	.024	.028	.025	.023	.034	.029	.032	.046	.023	.023	.016

NOTE: Rates are defined in the text.
[a] Primary central city.
[b] Suburbs.
[c] Other areas (see table 2.2).

relative to people in most of the central cities, imply higher numbers of vacant jobs in the central cities; but the rates and numbers of unemployed workers among residents in the central cities are much higher as well. Furthermore, the significant amount of commuting by suburban residents into the primary central cities suggests that many vacant jobs located in the central cities will not be filled by unemployed residents who live in them, thus raising the *effective* amount of central-city unemployment per vacant job.

Table 2.4 shows the ratios of numbers of filled jobs, vacant jobs, and unemployed workers to resident labor force participants in the primary central city versus the remainder of each metro area, using data from tables 1.1 and 1.2 for job locations and unemployment rates among residents and data from table 2.3 for job vacancy rates by location.[29] Each number is computed relative to the size of the labor force that resides in each location to adjust for differences in local population sizes and participation rates.[30] We also calculated "effective unemployment" in each location by applying commuting patterns observed among employed workers to the unemployed and reassigning locations for some of them on this basis.[31] The table also shows the differences between numbers of effectively unemployed workers and vacant jobs per labor force participant, as well as the ratios of unemployed workers to vacant jobs, for each location.[32]

These results reveal that, as we noted earlier, there are more

[29] Numbers of vacancies for each area are thus the vacancy rates multiplied by the numbers of filled jobs in each area, where the latter are computed from data on where people work in chapter 1.

[30] Since labor force participation rates are lower in the central cities than elsewhere, and since at least part of this gap seems likely to be attributable to differences in labor demand facing residents of the different areas, the use of labor force rather than population to adjust these figures will bias gaps in calculated unemployment between central cities and other parts of the metropolitan areas downward.

[31] In other words, we multiply the numbers of unemployed residents in each area by the fractions of working residents from those locations who work in the primary central city versus elsewhere in the area, and then reassign the unemployed on the basis of these "expected commute" patterns. This procedure assumes that the unemployed in each area will commute to the same extent as the employed residents there do, even though their average personal and labor market characteristics will differ. If anything, the resulting biases will likely be downward for unemployment rates in the central city, since it is among residents there that commuting patterns to the suburbs are most likely to be overstated.

[32] These are simply the arithmetic differences and ratios between the two, respectively.

Table 2.4 / Ratios of Filled Jobs, Vacancies, and Unemployed Workers

	Atlanta		Boston		Detroit		Los Angeles	
	PCC[a]	SUB/OTH[b]	PCC	SUB/OTH	PCC	SUB/OTH	PCC	SUB/OTH
Filled Jobs/LF	1.985	.786	1.472	.816	.842	.902	.938	.880
Vacancies/LF	.056	.020	.037	.021	.024	.032	.022	.019
Unemployed/LF	.092	.044	.068	.065	.197	.052	.084	.068
Effective Unemployed/LF	.127	.039	.108	.058	.134	.070	.082	.069
EU-V Gap/LF	.071	.019	.071	.037	.110	.038	.060	.050
EU/V	2.267	1.950	2.919	2.762	5.583	2.188	3.727	3.632

NOTE: "LF" refers to the labor force that resides in a particular area. "Effective Unemployment" is calculated by assigning commuting patterns of employed workers to the unemployed. "EU-V Gap" is the difference between the numbers of "Effective Unemployment" and Vacancies, while "EU/V" is the ratio of these two numbers.

[a] Primary central city.

[b] Suburbs and other areas, as defined in table 2.2.

jobs in the primary central cities per labor force participant than elsewhere in the metropolitan areas, except for Detroit. Similarly, the numbers of vacant jobs per participant in most of the central cities are higher than elsewhere, as are the numbers of unemployed workers per labor force participant (the unemployment rates).

The "effective unemployment" rate is higher than the conventionally measured rates for the central cities of Atlanta and Boston, but it is lower in Detroit and very similar in Los Angeles. The difference between the number of effectively unemployed workers and vacant jobs is clearly higher in each central city than in the corresponding suburban areas, while the ratios of the effectively unemployed to vacant jobs are higher in the central cities as well (though by a very small amount in Los Angeles).[33]

In Detroit, these gaps are particularly striking, with the number of unemployed workers per vacant job about two and a half times as large in the central city as in the remainder of the metropolitan area. Furthermore, it is very likely that these ratios would be much greater in the other central cities as well if we limited our analysis to areas in and around minority and/or low-income neighborhoods, where so many of the unemployed reside.

Overall, then, job availability per unemployed worker appears to be *lower* for unemployed residents in the central cities than in the suburbs. Despite the larger numbers of jobs relative to the populations of the central cities, the net in-commuting of suburban residents to central-city areas appears to eliminate any advantages that this might imply for the residents of the central cities. Of course, the locations of both employers and residents, along with the commuting flows between them, are not determined exogenously; they reflect the choices of various groups, given a set of costs and constraints that may be more severe for some than for others.[34] We will return to this subject in later chapters.

[33] Using actual rather than "effective" unemployment in these calculations would still show larger gaps between unemployment and vacancies in the central cities, though the ratios would be a bit lower in Atlanta and Boston.

[34] The "spatial mismatch" hypothesis is based on the notion that minorities face greater constraints on their choices of residential locations than whites do because of housing discrimination or segregation and that they also face potentially higher costs (or other difficulties) in commuting from central-city residences to suburban jobs. According to this idea, the result is a higher concentration of unemployed minorities relative to jobs in inner-city areas.

As we can see from table 2.5, professional/managerial and clerical vacancies generally account for more than half of the total number of job vacancies, especially in the central cities. Vacancies in the longest vacant jobs are concentrated in clerical jobs in the central cities, suggesting that there are particular difficulties in filling these positions.

Finally, we note that vacancy durations, which measure the time it takes for firms to fill available jobs, are generally comparable or higher in the primary central cities than in the suburbs. The gap between vacancy durations in the central cities and the suburbs is particularly high in Detroit, where the mean for the former is roughly double that for the latter.[35]

In general, vacancy durations should be inversely related to the frequency with which firms receive job applicants and the probabilities that these applicants are considered acceptable to the firm—both of which appear to be lower in occupations requiring greater skill. It is in this category in which vacancies appear to be relatively more concentrated in the central city. In addition, it is possible that the higher vacancy durations in the central city also reflect the relatively lower educational attainments and skill levels of applicants for these jobs among local residents, especially in Detroit.[36]

There is thus some evidence of differences between the central cities and the suburbs in both the relative availability of jobs and in the ease with which "job matches" are made. Differences only in relative job availability across areas or time periods should result in *negative* correlations between unemployment and vacancy rates; for example, in areas with larger quantities of unemployed job applicants, it should be easier for employers to fill job vacan-

[35] These data on durations of existing vacancies roughly parallel those for the durations of time it took to find the most recently hired workers in these firms. The numbers for current vacancies reflect durations of *incomplete* spells, while those for filled jobs reflect *completed* vacancy spells on a wider sample. The durations for filled jobs are significantly higher in the primary central cities than the suburbs for jobs not requiring college, and even more so for blue-collar and service jobs. These differences are only partly accounted for by skill requirements and/or 1-digit occupation dummies of jobs.

[36] See Holzer, Katz, and Krueger (1991) for a model and data on applicant rates to different firms and jobs. Barron, Berger, and Black (1994) present a model of vacancy durations. In equilibrium, firms might pay a somewhat higher wage to attract more/better workers, and thereby shorten vacancy durations caused by some "mismatch" between their skill requirements and those available in the local workforce.

Table 2.5 / Comparison of Job Vacancies by Occupation

	Atlanta			Boston			Detroit			Los Angeles		
	PCC	SUB	OTH	PCC	SUB	OTH	PCC	SUB	OTH	OCC	SUB	OTH
Occupations of All Vacancies												
Prof/Managerial	.261	.212	.194	.358	.343	.217	.273	.188	.275	.267	.259	.508
Sales	.142	.118	.091	.069	.123	.070	.071	.119	.151	.114	.160	.052
Clerical	.250	.113	.180	.220	.143	.279	.140	.139	.103	.263	.206	.171
Blue-collar	.210	.455	.427	.230	.218	.223	.203	.339	.340	.165	.200	.135
Other	.137	.102	.108	.124	.173	.211	.312	.214	.131	.191	.175	.135
Occupations of Longest Vacancies												
Prof/Managerial	.158	.120	.089	.120	.290	.078	.108	.134	.333	.100	.170	.222
Sales	.139	.173	.089	.160	.168	.098	.054	.114	.125	.080	.218	.111
Clerical	.455	.133	.267	.440	.229	.471	.487	.275	.125	.520	.265	.370
Blue-collar	.109	.373	.400	.180	.229	.118	.189	.301	.167	.200	.279	.148
Other	.139	.200	.157	.080	.084	.235	.167	.168	.208	.060	.068	.148
Duration of Longest Vacancy (Months)	1.405	1.322	1.397	1.676	1.901	2.028	3.632	1.804	1.669	2.337	1.739	4.214

NOTE: Columns under "Occupations" for each location sum to approximately one. "Longest Vacancy" refers only to jobs not requiring college.

cies. On the other hand, differences in the ease of "matching" workers to jobs should result in *positive* correlations between unemployment rates and vacancy rates/durations; where difficulties occur, both unemployed workers and vacant jobs will appear more plentiful and it will take longer to find successful matches.[37]

The higher ratios of effective unemployment to vacancies in the central cities of the metropolitan areas surveyed generally indicate decreased job availability for unemployed workers who live in them. Despite the much higher unemployment rates in the central cities, however, vacancy rates are comparable among them, and vacancy durations are longer in some of the central cities than elsewhere. This suggests that there are somewhat greater "mismatch" problems between unemployed workers and jobs in the central cities, likely reflecting employers' relatively higher skill requirements and/or lower skill levels in the local populations.

CHARACTERISTICS OF THE MOST RECENTLY FILLED JOBS

Aggregate data on hiring and vacancy rates reflect job turnover rates and the positions of labor markets in the business cycle. How these rates differ across industries, local areas, and/or occupations also tells us something about where new job availability is the greatest and perhaps where hiring difficulties are the most serious. But there are limitations to what we learn from these kinds of data, especially about job availability for the least-educated and least-skilled workers in the labor force.

It is therefore necessary to take a closer look at a representative sample of newly filled jobs in these labor markets, which should closely resemble a sample of all jobs that have been vacant over some recent period.[38] The characteristics of these jobs, such as

[37] This discussion is based on the idea of "Beveridge Curves," which plot unemployment and vacancy rates over time or across areas. See Abraham and Medoff (1982) for the former, and Holzer (1994a) for the latter. Theoretical justifications appear in Pissarides (1985), and in Blanchard and Diamond (1989). However, the applicability of these models to geographic differences within metropolitan areas is somewhat limited by the existence of commute flows between areas.

[38] Vacant jobs at any point in time will likely overrepresent those with long durations—jobs that are relatively hard to fill. In contrast, all jobs that have been vacant over a period of time will be more representative. The only differences between our sample of newly filled jobs and the one based on all vacant jobs in the recent past is that some of the jobs in our sample were likely filled without a period of job vacancy

the skills employers sought and the hiring criteria they used to fill them, will enable us to infer their availability to current job-seekers with the weakest skills and poorest credentials—those at the end of the "hiring queue" for most jobs.

Here and in subsequent chapters, we present data on the most recently filled jobs among firms that responded to our survey. We focus on jobs that do not require college degrees, though occasionally jobs that do require a college degree are included for the sake of comparison.

What we will be analyzing is an *employee-weighted sample of new jobs* across firms. Those employers that do a lot of hiring because of their large number of employees are heavily represented. On the other hand, firms that have many recent hires because of high turnover rates receive no extra weight. Thus, a single job in a firm that turns over frequently is still counted as a single job, since only a single available worker can fill that job at any given time.[39] This sample tends to overrepresent high-turnover jobs within firms, but the distributions of occupations in this sample resemble those for all workers in the metropolitan areas in the 1990 Census.

As the data in table 2.6 indicate, the vast majority of jobs that do not require a college degree are in the white-collar occupations, especially in the central cities.[40] Indeed, clerical jobs alone account for a third to a half of all these jobs in each of the central cities except in Detroit. In suburban areas, the fractions accounted for by clerical work are lower than in the central cities but still higher than in any other occupational category.

Professional/managerial jobs and sales jobs generally account for an additional 20–30 percent of non-college positions, with the former often higher in the central cities and the latter higher in the suburbs. Service occupations account for an additional 10–20

(in other words, the new employee was hired while the previous one occupied the job) and that the time periods in which the jobs were filled vary somewhat across firms.

[39] Unfortunately, firms that do a lot of hiring due to *net* employment growth do not receive any extra weight. The sample weights used here are only those (described in chapter 1) that correct for nonrandomness of firms generated by the household surveys.

[40] In this discussion, we define "white-collar" jobs as being the professional/managerial, clerical, and sales occupations. "Blue-collar" jobs are the craft, operative, and laborer occupations. Service occupations are not considered part of either group.

Table 2.6 / Occupations Requiring No College

	Atlanta			Boston			Detroit			Los Angeles		
	PCC[a]	SUB[b]	OTH[c]	PCC	SUB	OTH	PCC	SUB	OTH	PCC	SUB	OTH
Professional/Managerial	.150	.129	.128	.204	.139	.118	.167	.120	.174	.096	.137	.176
Sales	.200	.155	.198	.139	.185	.008	.079	.148	.138	.133	.134	.065
Clerical	.375	.252	.300	.386	.278	.368	.236	.274	.299	.480	.376	.362
Craft	.036	.088	.017	.025	.113	.078	.100	.110	.061	.064	.087	.076
Operative	.072	.160	.189	.059	.141	.186	.104	.127	.096	.116	.133	.141
Laborer	.034	.058	.039	.032	.038	.051	.059	.052	.042	.052	.034	.056
Service	.130	.152	.100	.148	.101	.116	.255	.161	.183	.059	.122	.122

[a] Primary central city.
[b] Suburbs.
[c] Other areas, as defined in table 2.2.

Table 2.7 / Wages and Benefits

	Atlanta			Boston		
	PCC[a]	SUB[b]	OTH[c]	PCC	SUB	OTH
No College Required						
Weekly Wage						
Mean	$326.83	$295.16	$289.86	$360.34	$331.63	$331.63
(Standard Deviation)	(142.04)	(133.29)	(131.04)	(153.73)	(157.01)	(184.53)
Median	320	280	280	386	324	321
Hourly Wage						
Mean	8.35	7.61	7.59	9.53	8.67	8.80
(Standard Deviation)	(3.28)	(2.74)	(3.30)	(3.39)	(3.10)	(3.64)
Median	7.94	7.00	6.99	9.40	8.17	8.15
Hourly Wage $6.00 or less	.231	.354	.383	.172	.231	.153
Benefits						
Own Health Insurance	.804	.740	.424	.866	.758	.782
Family Health Insurance	.680	.640	.483	.796	.705	.697
Employer Contributes to Pension	.577	.552	.494	.648	.487	.571
College Required						
Weekly Wage						
Mean	564.83	417.67	541.13	543.43	582.31	532.17
(Standard Deviation)	(188.96)	(173.29)	(128.93)	(189.05)	(288.76)	(199.20)
Median	576	481	519	519	481	568

[a] Primary central city.
[b] Suburbs.
[c] Other areas, as defined in table 2.2.

percent of non-college jobs, while blue-collar work accounts for just 10–20 percent of these jobs in the central city and 20–30 percent in suburbs. As noted above, these distributions closely resemble those observed in the 1990 Census for these metropolitan areas.[41]

[41] The published tabulations include college-educated workers, and thus show higher fractions of workers in professional/managerial jobs (27–36 percent) and somewhat lower ones in the clerical/sales/technical categories (33–38 percent) than those observed in our data. The fractions in the service and blue-collar occupations are comparable between the two data sources.

	Detroit			Los Angeles		
	PCC	SUB	OTH	PCC	SUB	OTH
No College Required						
Weekly Wage						
Mean	$288.41	$285.90	$262.33	$330.23	$322.88	$358.34
(Standard Deviation)	(154.05)	(176.32)	(162.57)	(149.10)	(177.78)	(270.45)
Median	279	260	245	320	300	300
Hourly Wage						
Mean	7.94	7.57	7.39	8.82	8.50	9.50
(Standard Deviation)	(4.25)	(3.35)	(3.93)	(3.55)	(3.75)	(5.15)
Median	7.00	7.00	6.50	8.20	7.99	7.82
Hourly Wage $6.00 or less	.432	.420	.311	.257	.324	.234
Benefits						
Own Health Insurance	.742	.729	.789	.711	.747	.822
Family Health Insurance	.693	.643	.673	.556	.627	.712
Employer Contributes to Pension	.587	.497	.509	.454	.486	.681
College Required						
Weekly Wage						
Mean	641.10	495.62	552.08	749.80	661.72	562.53
(Standard Deviation)	(245.77)	(177.79)	(259.93)	(550.27)	(875.48)	(511.34)
Median	586	532	481	538	514	512

What starting wages and benefits are available to workers on these jobs? For non-college jobs, we present means and medians for both hourly and weekly wages in table 2.7; for the sake of comparison, weekly wages are presented for jobs requiring college degrees as well. (See also table B.5 in appendix B.) For the non-college jobs, we also present the fractions of jobs paying $6.00 or less (which we arbitrarily classify as "low wages") and the fractions providing three major types of employee benefits: health insurance for the employee, health insurance for the employee's family, and employer contribution to pension funds.[42]

[42] We do not distinguish here between traditional pension plans and 401k plans.

A significant gap exists between the starting weekly wages of jobs that require a college degree and those that do not. The gap averages about 60–70 percent of the non-college wages in most locations, which is fairly comparable to the returns to college that have been observed in most other recent studies of the growing wage gaps between educational groups.[43]

Another striking finding is that, in most cases, wages for both college and non-college jobs in the primary central city are higher than are those in the suburbs. This may simply reflect a higher degree of skill required on jobs in the primary central city, even after controlling (as we do in a limited way) for educational requirements. Moreover, this finding is consistent with the notion that suburban residents must be compensated for their commute into the city, and perhaps also for certain other factors (the higher crime rate in the center city, for example). The higher occurrence of collective bargaining agreements in central-city jobs may also contribute to this result.

For jobs that do not require college degrees, the median starting hourly wage is in the $7.00–8.00 range in most locations. Therefore it is not surprising that 30–40 percent of these jobs pay $6.00 or less in most locations. Thus, substantial fractions of the available non-college jobs could be categorized as "low-wage" by this (admittedly arbitrary) standard.

Boston and Los Angeles are relatively high-wage areas compared to Atlanta and Detroit. Since the Atlanta and Detroit metropolitan areas contain many more blacks than do the Boston and Los Angeles metropolitan areas, part of any overall racial earnings differential that we observe will be caused by area differentials for which we must control (we will return to this point in chapter 5). We also note that the gap between central-city and suburban wages in Detroit for non-college jobs is the smallest of any observed here, which may also affect racial earnings gaps observed there.

Across industries, starting wages for non-college jobs in manufacturing remain well above those in retail trade but not much

[43] These data do not correspond exactly to those usually calculated with Current Population Survey data, since only starting wages are used here and since at least some people with college, including four-year degrees, are included here with the non-college group if they work in jobs that do not *require* college degrees.

more than those in the services; and, in the central city, manufacturing jobs often appear to pay less (see table B.5 in appendix B). This apparent weakening of the wage premium for manufacturing jobs, which traditionally have paid relatively well for less-educated workers, is a striking example of within-industry changes in the earnings structure that were likely caused by changes in the structure of labor demand in the previous few decades.[44]

Overall, about 70–80 percent of non-college jobs provide health insurance to employees;[45] a somewhat lower percentage provide them for family members; and roughly half or so provide employer contributions to pensions. Across locations and industries, the provision of these benefits appears to be positively correlated with starting wage levels. Thus, substantial fractions of new non-college jobs provide low wages as well as few employer benefits.

CONCLUSIONS

We may summarize our findings to this point by noting that most firms in the four metropolitan areas surveyed are in the retail trade, financial, and service sectors, while the majority of the newly filled non-college jobs are now white-collar (especially clerical) jobs. This is true in all locations but especially in the primary central cities, where blue-collar and manufacturing jobs are even less available than in the suburbs.

Median starting wages on non-college jobs are roughly $7.00–8.00 per hour, though substantial fractions of these jobs pay $6.00 or less and also provide no health care or employer contributions to pensions. Starting wages for both college and non-college jobs are generally higher in the central city than in the suburbs, though the magnitudes of these differences vary by metropolitan area.

[44] We would expect jobs in manufacturing to be more heavily affected by international trade than those in any other sector, and perhaps by technological changes as well. Earlier studies (for example, Freeman and Katz 1988; Revenga 1992; Lawrence and Slaughter 1993; Sachs and Shatz 1994) found relatively small effects of trade on wages in manufacturing, while Berman, Bound, and Griliches (1994) found that technological changes resulted in substantial within-industry changes in earnings.

[45] Whether employers actually *pay* for the health insurance in all of these cases is somewhat ambiguous.

With respect to job availability and the quantity of new hiring, we find that the fairly high gross hire rates at firms mostly reflect turnover rather than net employment growth. Despite the large amount of hiring that occurs, job vacancy rates are a good deal lower than unemployment rates overall, indicating that there is always some queuing of workers for jobs. But this seems to generate long periods of unemployment only for those workers near the back of the hiring queue, such as minorities and/or the less-educated (on whom we will focus in the remaining chapters).

Hiring and vacancy rates are lower in manufacturing than in other industries, likely reflecting differences in wages, turnover, and overall employment growth between these sectors. We also find that job vacancy *rates* are relatively comparable across primary central cities and the remainder of the metropolitan areas, while vacancy *durations* are comparable or somewhat higher in most of the central cities than elsewhere in the metropolitan areas.

The data on numbers of jobs and unemployment as well as on commuting patterns by area, and the comparable vacancy rates imply substantially higher ratios of unemployed residents to available vacant jobs in the central-city areas. Indeed, the ratio of unemployed workers to vacant jobs is two to three times higher in central-city Detroit than in the overall metropolitan area, indicating a dramatic shortage of jobs relative to unemployed workers there.

On the other hand, the comparable vacancy rates and higher vacancy durations in the primary central cities (at least in some locations), despite higher unemployment levels, suggest that some firms located there experience somewhat greater difficulties in the "matching" process than firms located elsewhere, although this may reflect their relatively higher skill requirements.

These issues will be explored at greater length in the following chapter, as we consider the skill requirements and hiring behavior of employers who are seeking to fill these jobs.

3 / What Skills Do Employers Seek and How Do They Seek Them?

The data presented in the previous chapter on hiring and job vacancy rates in major metropolitan areas and on some of the characteristics of the jobs that employers have recently filled lead us to ask the following questions: How many of these jobs are available to the less-educated and less-skilled workers in our major metropolitan areas? Are there enough jobs with low hiring requirements for workers in these areas who possess few skills and poor employment records?

These questions are at the heart of the debate among academics and policymakers regarding the degree to which we can expect the inner-city poor and minorities to find employment on their own in the private sector. These are also crucial questions in the current debate on welfare reform, particularly with respect to time limits on benefits; if time limits are set and welfare recipients are forced to seek work once the limits are reached, will these individuals be able to find employment on their own in the private sector? Or will governments have to engage in direct job creation (through subsidies to employers or public service employment)? The answers to these questions offered so far have been ambiguous, at least partly because of the paucity of data on employers and job characteristics.

In this chapter we hope to shed some light on these issues by looking more closely at the jobs that were recently filled by each employer in the survey and on employer behavior in filling them. Specifically, we will look at the skills needed to perform these jobs and at the recruiting and screening techniques used (and attitudes expressed) by employers.

Based on these data, we provide estimates of the fraction of jobs that might be accessible to those in the labor force with the lowest skills and least work experience. We show what fraction of jobs requires very few cognitive or interactive skills on a daily basis, and what fraction requires few serious credentials, such as previous experience, training, or references.

These estimates give us some measures of the *demand* for labor among those who possess very few skills. By comparing these fractions to certain estimates of the *supply* side of this market—the size of the low-skilled workforce in various locations, or potential increases in that workforce (caused, for instance, by the movement of recipients of Aid to Families with Dependent Children (AFDC) into the labor force due to welfare reform)—we can infer the relative degree of job availability that these workers face, at least in the short term. These data will therefore help to identify the seriousness of "mismatch" problems along skill lines and other dimensions, such as geographic location.[1] The wages paid on these jobs to various groups of workers will be considered in chapter 5.

All of these calculations are based on the fractions of recently filled jobs that fit into various categories based on skill requirements or employer hiring behavior. In comparing these numbers to the fractions of the population or labor force in similar categories, we make no inferences about the adequacy of the aggregate number of jobs relative to the number of people, only about the relative availability of these jobs for less-skilled workers.[2]

[1] A lack of job availability for the least-skilled could be caused by any wage rigidities that prevent these markets from fully equilibrating, whether resulting from minimum wages or the choices of employers themselves (as in the "efficiency wage" literature of macroeconomics (see Katz 1986)). Such a lack of job availability for specific labor market groups could occur even if the aggregate labor market appears to be close to equilibrium or to the "natural rate" of unemployment, as described in chapter 2.

[2] To the extent that an excess supply of workers over jobs exists in the aggregate (perhaps due to the business cycle) or in specific locations (such as some central cities), this comparison of fractions on the supply and demand sides of the labor market will actually *over*state job availability for the least-skilled groups.

Once again, we largely limited our sample to jobs that do not require employees to have four-year college degrees (though some employees, in fact, appear to have them). And as we noted in chapter 2, our sample consists of just one recently filled job for each firm in the survey. However, since our sample of firms is employee-weighted, it appears that we have generated a reasonably representative sample of the new jobs that jobseekers can expect to find.[3]

SKILL REQUIREMENTS

As we noted in chapter 1, recent research suggests that the growing inequality between workers in terms of earnings and employment is related to the increasing need of employers for workers with certain skills, even for jobs that do not require higher education. Indeed, some analysts (Wilson 1987; Kasarda 1995) allege that a "skill mismatch" (between the job requirements, on the one hand, and the availability of skills among inner-city workers, on the other) accounts for much of the high rate of nonemployment among minorities in the inner city.

Exactly what are the skills needed by employers for these jobs, and how intensively are they used? We measure the skill requirements of jobs by considering the frequency with which a variety of tasks—such as dealing with customers, either in person or on the phone; reading paragraphs; writing paragraphs; doing arithmetic calculations; and using computers—are performed.[4]

The tasks were chosen to represent the cognitive and social/interactive skills that are most frequently stressed in various policy-oriented discussions of the growing skill needs of employ-

[3]The distributions of overall employment by occupation (as well as of employees by race and gender) across the firms in our sample look roughly similar to the distributions across each variable for new hires. As noted in chapter 2, distributions of new hires by occupation and industry also resemble those that are based on Bureau of Labor Statistics surveys and the 1990 Census.

[4]We note that there is some ambiguity about exactly what constitutes use of a "computer," and that great variation may exist in the skills needed to do so. For instance, the use of computerized scanners at checkout counters in supermarkets might be an example of computer use that requires little skill. More generally, it is well known that new capital and technology can either complement or substitute for worker skills, though on average the former effect appears to dominate (Hamermesh 1993; Bartel and Lichtenberg 1987).

ers.[5] The results of our survey (table 3.1) show that each of these tasks (except one) is performed daily in half or more of jobs that do not require a college degree. Indeed, arithmetic is performed daily in 65 percent of these jobs, while the exception (writing paragraphs) is performed daily in 30 percent. In contrast, most workers who do not perform these tasks daily do not perform them at all.

This relatively high frequency of cognitive and social task performance is found despite the overrepresentation in our survey of high-turnover jobs within firms. It also no doubt reflects the occupational composition of our sample, with its large fraction of clerical, sales, and service workers (see chapter 2).

To avoid the effects of occupational composition on our overall measures of task performance, we computed the fraction of jobs in which each of the above tasks is performed daily for each of the major occupational categories.[6] Separate estimates are also provided for each of the three types of geographic areas: primary central cities, suburban areas, and "other" areas (other central cities and municipal areas with blacks accounting for at least 30 percent of their residential populations).

As might be expected, and as the data in table 3.2 confirm, professional/managerial and clerical employees perform all of these tasks with relatively high degrees of frequency. Sales employees show an even greater degree of contact with customers and performance of arithmetic calculations.

But task performance rates are fairly high even in the non-white-collar job categories. Service employees, who are generally in the lowest wage categories, deal with customers daily in the great majority of cases, and 50–60 percent must read or write paragraphs and make arithmetic calculations. Among employees who are in crafts or are operatives (i.e., operators of equipment), the daily performance of the last two tasks is comparable to that observed among service workers, while among laborers the rate of customer contact and reading and writing is fairly low, com-

[5] See, for instance, Barton and Kirsch (1990), or Packer and Wirt (1992).

[6] Dealing with customers by telephone or in person is a single category here, as is the reading or writing of paragraphs. In these combined categories, performance of one or the other of the tasks can constitute a daily performance for the combined category.

Table 3.1 / Task Performance Frequency on Non-College Jobs

	Daily	Once a Week	Once a Month	Not at All
Deal with Customers				
In Person	.581	.068	.024	.326
On Telephone	.531	.070	.020	.379
Read Paragraphs	.549	.206	.071	.175
Write Paragraphs	.299	.168	.096	.436
Do Arithmetic	.649	.122	.042	.182
Use Computers	.510	.052	.023	.415

pared to the performance of arithmetic calculations, which is somewhat higher. Only use of computers appears infrequently for all of the non-white-collar occupations.

Furthermore, task-performance rates are generally a bit higher in the primary central-city areas, even after controlling for occupational category. Based on the tabulations of occupation by area from chapter 2, it is clear that these gaps would be even larger if they were not computed within occupation. Thus, the cognitive and interactive skills needed for daily task performance in non-college jobs appear to be substantial, even in non-white-collar jobs and especially in central-city areas. These findings also appear to be consistent with other studies that have surveyed the skill requirements of newly available jobs.[7]

RECRUITMENT

If employers need to find skilled workers to fill their available jobs, how do they go about recruiting applicants for these positions? Some recruitment methods (such as the use of private employment agencies or newspaper advertisements) are more costly than others for employers, but these methods may be more effective in generating the higher-quality applicants (or those with specialized skills) that some employers need.[8]

[7] See, for instance, the discussion of the SCANS report from the U.S. Department of Labor in Packer and Wirt (1992). Kasarda (1995) has argued that skill needs on jobs in the central city have grown particularly, due to the loss of manufacturing jobs there and the growth of "information-processing" employment.

[8] A model that allows employers to choose among alternative recruitment procedures based on their relative benefits and costs can be found in Holzer (1987a). Some

Table 3.2 / Daily Task Performance on Non-College Jobs

	Dealing w/Customers			Reading/Writing			Arithmetic			Computers		
	PCC[a]	SUB[b]	OTH[c]	PCC	SUB	OTH	PCC	SUB	OTH	PCC	SUB	OTH
Professional/Managerial	.801	.716	.770	.824	.805	.735	.776	.696	.699	.666	.582	.540
Sales	.962	.960	.950	.609	.617	.457	.818	.819	.857	.660	.668	.559
Clerical	.861	.775	.721	.711	.664	.549	.629	.653	.641	.812	.770	.753
Craft	.354	.458	.445	.545	.586	.574	.477	.645	.695	.182	.208	.137
Operative	.528	.327	.383	.543	.496	.436	.644	.607	.546	.280	.242	.138
Laborer	.348	.273	.386	.396	.277	.403	.456	.521	.612	.119	.183	.098
Service	.706	.765	.861	.585	.551	.554	.502	.494	.571	.165	.188	.317

[a] Primary central city.
[b] Suburbs.
[c] Other areas, as defined in table 2.2.

Among the less costly methods of recruiting workers, it has long been argued that referrals from informal sources (such as current employees) on average generate better-quality employees and more honest information for employers than do more formal referral sources. On the other hand, heavy employer reliance on informal networks may disadvantage minorities, especially those from low-income families or neighborhoods that are "socially isolated" and where few working adults are present.[9]

State employment services might generate a larger quantity of applicants for employers and are more easily accessible to lower-income people, but the quality of applicants generated appears to be a good deal more suspect from the employer's point of view.

Our data on the recruitment methods that generated the most recently hired non-college employee in the firms surveyed are presented in table 3.3 and table 3.4. Generally, the method that most frequently generates new employees is newspaper advertising, which accounts for 25–30 percent of those hired. Referral through current employees generates almost as many employees, or roughly 25 percent. Indeed, if referrals from current employees were combined with those from other informal sources (such as acquaintances of the employer), such informal referral mechanisms would account for 35–40 percent of new hires. Furthermore, even some of the other recruitment mechanisms (such as schools or even walk-ins) undoubtedly involve networks or contacts on the employee side.[10]

In contrast, less than a fifth of jobs are filled by walk-ins without referrals and applicants responding to help-wanted signs. Employers use private employment agencies for roughly 5–10 percent

---

data are also presented there on recruitment and screening from an earlier survey of employers.

[9]The argument about the quality of information obtainable from private referral sources and state employment services was first made among economists by Rees (1966), and now appears in many human resources (or personnel) texts. See Holzer (1987a), Fernandez (1991), and Pedder (1991) for discussion and evidence on the potential disadvantage to minorities caused by employer reliance on informal methods of recruitment, and Wilson (1987) for the "social isolation" hypothesis, more generally.

[10]These numbers are consistent with those that appear in my earlier work (1987a), in which 35–40 percent of workers in the National Longitudinal Survey of Youth claim to have obtained employment through friends and relatives. Data from the Panel Survey of Income Dynamics, where the sample is household heads and where the survey questions refer even more broadly to use of contacts, imply that over half of employees obtain their jobs in this manner (Corcoran, Datcher, and Duncan 1980).

Table 3.3 / Recruitment Methods for Last Employee Hired in Non-College Job

	Primary Central City	Suburbs	Other Areas[a]
Newspaper	.240	.295	.290
Help-Wanted Sign	.042	.047	.042
Walk-In (No referral)	.142	.131	.148
Referral From			
Current Employees	.259	.253	.258
State Employment Service	.018	.033	.051
Private Employment Service	.096	.044	.052
Community Agency	.034	.010	.011
Schools	.034	.046	.025
Union	.012	.008	.062
Other (acquaintances, etc.)	.124	.134	.117
Used Affirmative Action in Recruiting	.583	.517	.588

NOTE: Only one method was used to generate each employee. Each column sums to (approximately) one.
[a] As defined in table 2.2.

of their hires (more in the primary central city than elsewhere) and state employment offices, a mechanism designed specifically for use by the less skilled, for 5 percent or less of their hires (less in the primary central city than elsewhere).[11]

As one might expect, the method of recruitment used to generate the most recent hire also varies by occupational category (table 3.4). Help-wanted signs and walk-ins are used somewhat more frequently for sales and service positions (presumably in retail trade establishments), and newspapers are used somewhat more frequently for professional/managerial and clerical jobs than for others. Private employment services are also used a bit more frequently in clerical jobs.

In contrast, employers in the blue-collar occupations rely even more heavily than do others on referrals from current employees and (to a much lesser extent) on the state employment services. The importance of informal networks thus appears to be relatively

[11] See Rees (1966) for an earlier appraisal of the limited use of state employment services in the United States. Rees argued that the service was, in fact, stigmatized by its referrals of less-skilled workers, and that private referral sources generate better-quality applicants as well as more reliable information.

Table 3.4 / Recruitment by Occupation

	Prof/Mgt.	Sales	Clerical	Craft	Operative	Laborer	Service
Newspaper	.345	.237	.332	.248	.241	.124	.260
Help-Wanted Sign	.023	.104	.025	.009	.027	.024	.097
Walk-In	.076	.200	.112	.086	.176	.119	.180
Referral From							
Current Employees	.252	.192	.229	.310	.279	.447	.266
State Employment Service	.024	.010	.030	.024	.078	.092	.013
Private Employment Service	.057	.052	.083	.031	.065	.060	.007
Community Agency	.010	.011	.023	.030	.010	.027	.012
Schools	.065	.028	.053	.040	.014	.009	.026
Union	.006	.005	.006	.033	.005	.000	.009
Other (acquaintances, etc.)	.142	.162	.108	.190	.106	.096	.130
Used Affirmative Action in Recruiting	.545	.460	.658	.398	.490	.466	.534

greater in the sectors in which fewer cognitive and social skills are required for work, and perhaps where more basic issues of personal behavior (for example, a lack of absenteeism) are of relatively greater concern to employers.

It therefore appears that jobseekers with few personal contacts in the working world (such as residents of high-poverty neighborhoods and/or members of households with no employed adults) may well face serious barriers in obtaining the available jobs for non-college graduates in significant numbers, as the "social isolation" hypothesis suggests. These difficulties are especially serious for those interested in finding blue-collar work.

Between 50 and 60 percent of respondents said they followed affirmative action policies in their recruitment procedures. Exactly what these were was not specified, and whether this practice affected the likelihood of females and/or minorities being hired will be addressed in a later chapter.

SCREENING

Once applicants have been recruited, they must be screened to determine the most suitable candidate for an available position. In effect, employers try to predict the prospective future performance of these candidates in the job. Employers choose a set of hiring requirements that they believe "signal" a candidate's potential suitability and engage in various activities that might help them to gain more information about a candidate's qualifications. Again, some of these screens may act as greater barriers for minority candidates than for others at the hiring stage.[12]

Our survey (table 3.5) revealed that applicants for non-college jobs must pass through a fairly large number of screens in order to be hired. For instance, roughly three-quarters of available jobs require high school diplomas. Roughly 70 percent of these non-college jobs require some general work experience and about 73

[12] See Holzer (1987a) for more discussion of screening mechanisms in general. Economic models in which employers choose specific signals of applicant quality (and where employees may be able to "invest" in certain signals, such as education) can be found in Spence (1973) or Thurow (1979). The fact that these signals may disproportionately hurt black applicants, even those who are qualified, appears in these models and also in the models of "statistical discrimination" (reviewed in Cain 1986). More evidence is presented on this issue in chapter 4.

Table 3.5 / Screening Methods for Non-College Jobs

	Primary Central City	Suburbs	Other Areas[a]
Requirements for Hiring			
High School Diploma	.761	.704	.684
General Experience	.722	.671	.672
Specific Experience	.667	.596	.582
References	.735	.721	.728
Vocational or Other Training	.417	.388	.310
Other Screening Activities			
Test/Physical	.180	.163	.185
Test/Other	.572	.453	.498
Check Education	.348	.257	.270
Check Criminal Record	.336	.292	.385
Interview	.874	.874	.852
Used Affirmative Action in Hiring	.421	.368	.428

NOTE: The criteria presented here were considered to be requirements for hiring only if an employer said they were "absolutely necessary" or "strongly preferred." The screening activities were counted only if an employer said they were "always" used.
[a] As described in table 2.2.

percent require references. Specific experience (in the particular job category) is required in over 60 percent of these jobs, while previous vocational education or other kinds of training are required in roughly 40 percent.

Tests (other than physical ones) are used as a screening mechanism in roughly half of all non-college jobs. Checks on education or criminal activity are conducted in roughly 30–40 percent of all cases, and interviews are conducted 85–90 percent of the time. Affirmative action comes into play roughly 40 percent of the time.

Overall, the number of screens employed for non-college jobs is somewhat higher in primary central-city areas than elsewhere. Table 3.6 shows that, across occupations, there is considerable variance in their use as well. In general, employers trying to fill operative, laborer, or service jobs have fewer hiring requirements and use fewer screens than employers in other categories.

Nevertheless, even in the less-skilled occupational categories the hiring screens appear to be fairly substantial. For instance, specific experience is required for more than half of operative and service jobs, and previous training is required for a third of them

Table 3.6 / Screening Methods by Occupation

	Prof./Mgt.	Sales	Clerical	Craft	Operative	Laborer	Service
Requirements for Hiring							
High School Diploma	.859	.699	.865	.599	.485	.507	.594
General Experience	.758	.663	.731	.724	.620	.567	.605
Specific Experience	.800	.542	.627	.716	.550	.338	.554
References	.827	.736	.721	.653	.662	.659	.753
Vocational or Other Training	.578	.262	.375	.556	.341	.245	.334
Other Screening Activities							
Test/Physical	.151	.091	.178	.171	.317	.181	.130
Test/Other	.507	.322	.586	.536	.517	.309	.450
Check Education	.375	.270	.300	.208	.176	.195	.346
Check Criminal Record	.338	.308	.342	.217	.217	.260	.416
Interview	.902	.856	.888	.853	.816	.819	.890
Used Affirmative Action in Hiring	.444	.306	.468	.264	.336	.344	.374

(with somewhat less experience and training required for laborer positions). Non-physical tests are also required for roughly half of these jobs.

It is possible that employers are overstating the extent to which they demand various credentials and that they settle for less under some circumstances (such as in tight labor markets). In the next chapter we will consider the extent to which these reported screens and criteria affect the demographics of who gets hired, thus determining the extent to which these self-reported measures affect actual behavior.

Although screening procedures no doubt have important effects on who gets hired into various jobs, more subjective factors, such as employer attitudes, may play a role as well. Indeed, the fact that almost 90 percent of applicants face some type of interview indicates that most employers want an opportunity to judge their applicants personally in a format in which they can go beyond the information obtained from more objective measures.

We therefore consider two types of measures of employer attitudes and preferences: (1) whether employers would "definitely" or "probably" hire someone for this position with some potentially stigmatizing personal characteristic, such as being a welfare recipient, having a General Equivalence Degree (GED) or experience in a government training program, having only short-term or part-time work experience, having been unemployed for a year or more, or having a criminal record;[13] and (2) whether employers consider it "very important" or "somewhat important" for the applicant to show attractive physical appearance or neatness, good English/verbal skills, politeness, or motivation in an interview.[14] These attributes have been stressed in studies that focus on so-called "soft skills" (see Moss and Tilly 1993), though little has been done to date to try to quantify such measures and their effects on the hiring process.

[13] The survey questions did not specify that applicants with these characteristics would be otherwise qualified. We hoped to gauge employer impressions of these candidates, and what expected qualifications they would attach to such individuals on their own.

[14] The questions in the latter category were asked and responses are presented only for those employers who said that they use interviews "always" or "sometimes" as a hiring screen.

Self-reported measures of such subjective factors may be difficult to interpret and are no doubt marred by significant "error" in a statistical sense.[15] Nevertheless, employer responses to such questions may still tell us something about employers' preferences in a broad sense that could have important implications for who gets hired into various kinds of non-college jobs.

In table 3.7, our data reveal that 80–85 percent of employers claim that they would hire welfare recipients or applicants with GEDs and/or government training. On face value, these results imply that little stigma is attached to these characteristics per se. Of course, it is possible that these responses (especially on welfare recipiency) are biased upward, if they are viewed by employers as the "politically correct" answers.[16] Furthermore, the roughly 80 percent of employers who would hire GEDs and/or government trainees is comparable to the fraction who reported that they required high school diplomas.[17]

As for other characteristics, just over two-thirds of employers claim that they would hire someone with a year or more of unemployment recently. But less than half would be willing to hire applicants with only short-term or part-time work experience, and just about a third would hire someone with a criminal record.

The reluctance of employers to hire someone with a spotty work history revealed in our survey is consistent with evidence on the hiring behavior of inner-city employers that has appeared elsewhere (Ballen and Freeman 1986).[18] Early employment insta-

[15] Random measurement error in these responses would imply that the means presented in this table are unbiased but that estimated relationships between these factors and employment outcomes (considered in the next chapter) would be biased toward zero. If the error is systematic rather than random, the reported means might also be biased in one direction or another.

[16] It is not obvious why "political correctness" would be more of a consideration on these questions than on others we consider. One reason might be that welfare recipiency is more highly correlated with race in employers' minds than are some of these other characteristics, and negative answers may not be considered as acceptable as they are with other attributes, such as criminal activity.

[17] Whether individuals with a GED are actually considered "perfect substitutes" for those with a high school diploma is not clear here and would no doubt depend on other characteristics and skills that these individuals brought to the employer. For other evidence on this question, see Cameron and Heckman (1993) and Murnane (1993).

[18] They found that repeated short employment spells among young blacks do not reduce the lengthy durations of subsequent spells of nonemployment. Interviews they

Table 3.7 / Employer Attitudes and Preferences with Respect to Non-College Jobs

	Primary Central City	Suburbs	Other Areas[a]
Would Hire			
Welfare Recipient	.819	.843	.855
GED/Government Trainee	.818	.795	.789
Only Part-Time or Short-Term Experience	.477	.493	.478
Unemployment of at Least One Year	.684	.677	.675
Criminal Record	.332	.348	.305
Important Interview Factors			
Physical Appearance/Neatness	.555	.524	.504
English/Verbal Skills	.784	.687	.647
Politeness	.811	.765	.749
Motivation	.753	.728	.746

NOTE: Employers included among those who "would hire" each type of applicant are those who indicated they would "definitely accept" or "probably accept" such an applicant for this position. Interview factors were counted only if an employer indicated that each was "very important" or "somewhat important."
[a] As described in table 2.2.

bility may also impede wage growth as well as employment for workers in their later years.[19] Furthermore, since many welfare recipients or candidates with GEDs and/or government training often bring these attributes to the labor market, their expected success may be greatly diminished by these factors.

The expressed antipathy of employers toward those with criminal records is also interesting in light of the fact that most employers do *not* check criminal records.[20] This suggests that, for em-

conducted with small employers in Roxbury (a predominantly black and low-income area in Boston) indicated a reluctance to hire people with unstable work histories, which was consistent with their statistical evidence.

[19] Meyer and Wise (1982) and Ellwood (1982) both argue that the primary effect of early youth unemployment is on workers' wages rather than their future employment, which is consistent with the idea that the primary effect is in lost working experience. On the other hand, Rich (1994) provides evidence of effects on future employment from more recent data.

[20] Doing so may, in fact, be difficult and time-consuming, as the exact institution where such information would be publicly available is not always obvious. Questions about the relevant jurisdiction (local versus state or federal) may compound these difficulties.

ployers, the mere suspicion of criminal activity or incarceration (perhaps from major gaps in a job candidate's work history) may be enough to preclude an applicant from being hired, and it is highly likely that such suspicions would be directed most strongly against young black male job candidates, especially poorly educated ones or those from low-income neighborhoods. Therefore, the finding elsewhere (Freeman 1992) that those who do, in fact, participate in criminal activity and become incarcerated suffer significantly more joblessness in subsequent years than those who do not may be at least partly attributable to employer hiring attitudes and behavior, as well as to employers' ability to at least partially predict who has engaged in such behavior.[21]

With respect to the factors employers weight most heavily in interviews, we find that physical appearance or neatness were considered to be important for just over half of the recently filled non-college jobs, while English/verbal skills were considered to be so for roughly 70 percent. Demonstrations of politeness and motivation were stressed 70–80 percent of the time.

We find some limited variance in these measures across geographic areas and across occupational categories (table 3.8). Thus, some of the interview factors (especially English/verbal skills and politeness) are more heavily weighted by employers in primary central cities and in sales, service, and clerical jobs.[22] It is striking that employer willingness to hire welfare recipients, those with unstable work histories, and those with criminal records varies little across occupational categories.

One interpretation of this finding is that employers read these factors as signals of general employability and readiness for work, rather than as measures of specific skills that may be more or less necessary for specific kinds of work. But regardless of the exact reason, the uniformity with which these attitudes are found across occupations suggests that those who have (or are suspected of having) criminal records or unstable work histories will have dif-

[21] Alternative explanations for this finding include choices made by the workers themselves to participate less consistently in the labor market. Evidence on this issue by Grogger (1993) is less clear about whether the long-term employment effects of criminal activity and incarceration really reflect these factors rather than unobserved personal characteristics.

[22] In fact, occupational composition of jobs seems to account for most of the differences in these measures across the geographic areas.

Table 3.8 / Employer Attitudes and Preferences

	Prof./Mgt.	Sales	Clerical	Craft	Operative	Laborer	Service
Would Hire							
Welfare Recipient	.854	.761	.856	.780	.853	.886	.872
GED/Government Trainee	.812	.807	.805	.798	.814	.804	.784
Only Part-Time or Short-Term Experience	.492	.490	.501	.433	.464	.509	.494
Unemployment of at Least One Year	.716	.667	.697	.653	.674	.686	.651
Criminal Record	.344	.279	.299	.396	.419	.449	.332
Important Interview Factors							
Physical Appearance/Neatness	.522	.645	.567	.375	.318	.297	.687
English/Verbal Skills	.765	.871	.821	.511	.429	.396	.676
Politeness	.782	.925	.838	.628	.530	.500	.861
Motivation	.802	.799	.722	.744	.651	.659	.732

ficulty being hired in even the lowest-wage and least skill-intensive sectors of the economy.

JOB AVAILABILITY FOR THE LEAST SKILLED

What do these data tell us about the availability of work for those in our society who have the lowest skill levels, the worst credentials, and the least experience in the labor force? Are jobs actually available at some wage for all who really want to work, as some (see, for example, Mead 1992) allege? Of more immediate policy significance, will all AFDC recipients who are required to work at the end of some specified time period really be able to obtain such work fairly quickly, if no wage subsidies or other public-sector job creation efforts are undertaken?

These questions lie at the heart of the debate about whether low employment rates among the less-skilled are due to external constraints on the demand side of the labor market or choices by workers on the supply side, and the evidence on these matters so far has provided few definitive answers. But since the data analyzed here clearly focus on the demand side of the market, they provide more direct evidence on job availability for the least-skilled than have the more traditional data from the supply side.

Non-college jobs that apparently require very few skills or credentials by job applicants are the jobs that are presumably obtainable by those (such as long-term AFDC recipients) who have very little if any recent work experience or training, few or no references, and show little sign of strong cognitive or interactive skills. We have calculated the fractions of non-college jobs that require none of the tasks described earlier in this chapter to be performed daily, as well as those where only talking to customers (in person or over the phone) daily is required. We also have calculated the fractions of jobs that require neither a high school diploma, general or specific work experience, references, nor previous training. Alternatively, we have calculated those that only require a high school diploma, or a high school diploma and some general work experience.

The results of table 3.9 show that very few of the available non-college jobs require no daily cognitive/social task performance or no credentials at the hiring stage. More specifically, only

Table 3.9 / Percentages of Non-College Jobs That Require Few Tasks and Little Screening by Location

	Primary Central City	Suburbs	Other Areas[a]
Perform None of Major Tasks Daily	.056	.084	.100
Perform None of Tasks Except Talking to Customers	.103	.142	.153
Requires No High School Diploma, Training, Experience, or References	.041	.061	.054
Requires Only High School Diploma	.067	.091	.075
Requires Only High School Diploma and General Experience	.095	.125	.110

[a] As defined in table 2.2.

5–10 percent require none of the daily tasks, and just 4–6 percent require none of the credentials. If we broaden our definition of low-skill jobs to include those whose only requirement is that the employee deal with customers (but which require no real cognitive task performance), the portion of non-college jobs available rises to 10–15 percent of the total jobs available. If we allow for applicants who have high school diplomas (but no other credentials), the portion rises to 7–9 percent, and if we allow for those with high school diplomas and at least some general experience, the portion rises to 10–13 percent.

It is clear that even fewer of the non-college jobs located in primary central-city areas are available to the least-skilled than are available in suburban areas. For instance, only 5.6 percent of these jobs in the primary central cities require no daily tasks, and only 4.1 percent require none of the credentials, compared to 8.4 percent and 6.1 percent of the jobs, respectively, in the suburbs.

It is theoretically possible that the *number* of such jobs available in the central cities is comparable to or greater than the number elsewhere, even though the *fraction* that they constitute of all non-college jobs is lower, but the data on job vacancies and unemployment in the previous chapter clearly suggest that this is not the case. Furthermore, if an excess supply of workers over jobs exists in the central cities, or even in the labor market overall (as the comparisons of unemployment and vacancy rates in chapter 2 suggest), these comparisons of the relevant fractions of workers and jobs would *over*state job availability to the least-educated workers in both locations, but especially in the central cities.

Across occupations (table 3.10), we find that jobs requiring no tasks and no credentials are in very short supply in the white-collar job categories, and the data from chapter 2 imply that white-collar jobs now constitute 60–70 percent of all recently filled jobs for non-college workers. Even among service jobs, only about 20 percent require no daily tasks other than dealing with customers, and only about 10 percent require no credentials other than a high school diploma. These percentages rise somewhat for traditional blue-collar jobs, especially those for laborers; but even in this latter (small) category, just under 40 percent of jobs require no daily tasks, and just over 20 percent require no credentials other than a high school diploma. Thus, even the high rates of future job growth projected for some low-skill occupational categories do not necessarily imply an abundance of jobs without major skill requirements.[23]

Since these numbers reflect only the demand side of the labor market, we must compare them to those on the supply side to get a real sense of the relative availability of such jobs for all who might want or need them. Although all of the numbers are not available, it is possible to make a few instructive comparisons.

For instance, high school dropouts constitute roughly 20 percent of the overall population and about 25 percent of the population without college degrees. The numbers are somewhat lower among younger age groups and in major metropolitan areas (Mare 1995; Hauser and Phang 1993). When compared to the fractions of non-college jobs that require high school diplomas, these numbers alone indicate an approximate aggregate balance between job availability and people without high school degrees.

However, dropout rates for those residing in central-city areas (unadjusted for other personal characteristics) are 50 percent

[23]The computed fractions of jobs with few skill requirements are no doubt lowered by job measures that implicitly weight firms by the numbers of employees rather than the numbers of gross hires; but the former weights are probably more appropriate. If anything, the overrepresentation of high-turnover jobs within firms here probably biases our estimates of relative employer skill needs downward. On the other hand, this sample no doubt misses the many low-skill jobs in the "informal sector" of the economy, though this is true of Bureau of Labor Statistics and census surveys as well.

Table 3.10 / Percentages of Non-College Jobs That Require Few Tasks and Little Screening by Occupation

	Prof./Mgt.	Sales	Clerical	Craft	Operative	Laborer	Service
Perform None of Major Tasks Daily	.023	.003	.036	.156	.180	.310	.103
Perform None of Tasks, Except Talking to Customers	.067	.054	.076	.226	.223	.380	.208
Requires No High School Diploma, Training, Experience, or References	.015	.054	.027	.055	.102	.149	.082
Requires Only High School Diploma	.024	.101	.054	.080	.131	.181	.105
Requires Only High School Diploma and General Experience	.044	.136	.088	.098	.183	.230	.128

higher among whites and nearly 100 percent higher among blacks than for those residing in other parts of large metropolitan areas (Hauser and Phang 1993). In contrast, the fraction of jobs available to these individuals is somewhat lower in the central city, as we have seen.

If we had additional data on the numbers of people with certain cognitive abilities, levels of work experience or training, and the like, we would no doubt find similar patterns of central-city residents lagging behind suburban residents with respect to each of these credentials. Furthermore, the fractions of individuals who are lacking at least one of these credentials would no doubt be higher than the fraction lacking education only, while the fraction of jobs accessible to these people would be lower with each additional criterion considered (assuming that all of the criteria must be met for someone to be hired). Thus, it is highly likely that the fraction of people in the central-city areas without the needed education, experience, and training substantially exceeds the small fraction of jobs in those areas that require few of these credentials and skills.

Of course, this imbalance between low-skill job availability and residents in the central-city would be irrelevant if the latter could easily travel across geographic areas to work (or search for work). Indeed, a significant number of people commute from the suburbs to central cities and from central cities to the suburbs. But for low-income central-city residents without access to automobiles and without a great deal of information about (or contacts in) suburban communities, the opportunities for finding jobs there and commuting are greatly diminished. Indeed, most of these people look for jobs and work in the central city.[24]

IMPLICATIONS FOR WELFARE REFORM

These same conditions will confront AFDC recipients who will be required to seek employment under pending welfare reform

[24] This idea of costly commuting, or even barriers that limit such activity, underlies much of the "spatial mismatch" literature (Holzer 1991; Kain 1992). Direct evidence on low rates of commuting (while working or searching for work) among central-city residents can be found in Holzer, Ihlanfeldt, and Sjoquist (1994), and in Farley, Holzer, and Danziger (1995). It is important to note again that even parts of the primary central cities may not be accessible to people from very low-income neighborhoods.

legislation. Two to three million women would be added to the labor force during the next several years under most current proposals for welfare reform.[25] As a fraction of the overall U.S. labor force (131 million, of whom 58 million are women), the net addition looks relatively small.

However, these new labor force entrants will certainly not be competing with all other workers for available jobs. Among other things, AFDC recipients are concentrated geographically. Indeed, various estimates suggest that they constitute 15–20 percent of heads of households in the largest cities (in New York and Chicago, for example) and over 20 percent in a few places (such as in Detroit).[26] If most new labor force entrants from the welfare rolls in these cities search for employment within the boundaries of the central city, the net additions to the local labor force will ultimately be quite substantial.

Furthermore, these new entrants will be very heavily concentrated among the least-skilled workers. The data indicate that 48–70 percent of *long-term* AFDC recipients are high school dropouts; most do poorly on tests of cognitive ability; 30–40 percent had no recent work experience when they began to receive aid; most will be unable or unwilling to cite work experience as aid recipients; and 50–65 percent are black.[27]

Most of these women entering the labor force will therefore be competing for the very small fraction of available jobs in the central cities that have few serious requirements in terms of skills and credentials, and where there is currently no evidence of any

[25] There are roughly 5 million families on AFDC currently; Danziger and Weinberg (1994) report about 3.3 million in 1989, and the number has grown considerably since then. About 40 percent of those currently on AFDC have been recipients for at least five years or more (Bane and Ellwood 1994), and they would be terminated from the program entirely; many others will be induced to join the labor force even before the five-year limit is reached.

[26] See, for instance, Wacquant and Wilson (1989) for evidence on several large cities, and Farley, Holzer, and Danziger (1995) for Detroit.

[27] Education, recent work experience, and race of long-term recipients are calculated from Bane and Ellwood (1994, chapter 2). The lower numbers in the various ranges reported here reflect the fractions of all individuals currently on AFDC, a sample that overrepresents long-term spells; the higher numbers in each range are the fractions of all recipients with spells at least ten years long who fit into each category. Burtless (1995) also reports that 72 percent of women with twelve consecutive months of welfare dependency score in the bottom quartile of all young people on Armed Forces Qualifying Tests, according to tabulations from the National Longitudinal Survey of Youth.

shortage of workers. Nonemployment spells among young black males and females in inner-city areas are already very lengthy, even among those who are not in school and who participate in the labor force; unemployment rates for less-educated men and women more generally are quite high; and very significant periods of nonemployment are currently observed among poor single female heads of households, even when they are not receiving aid.[28] It is hard to imagine that *all* such nonemployment is accounted for by the choices made by the workers on the supply side of the labor market themselves; presumably at least some of it occurs because of shortfalls in job offers (or labor demand) as well.[29] Moreover, these employment difficulties for minorities and the least-skilled are apparent at all points in the business cycle, even when the labor markets appear to be relatively tight.[30]

Thus, it is highly likely that a fairly large fraction of current long-term AFDC recipients who will be required to enter the labor force will likely be unable to find work in the short term, especially if they receive no special training and in the absence of public job-creation efforts (such as subsidies for their employment in the private sector or direct public-sector employment).

In the longer term, the labor market may adjust to this influx of less-skilled workers with the creation of more jobs, perhaps at

[28] Average nonemployment durations of as much as a year for out-of-school black male and female teens have been calculated by Clark and Summers (1982), and Ballen and Freeman (1986) for the 1970s and early 1980s, while Juhn *et al.* (1991) have found growing durations of nonemployment recently for the lowest-wage workers. Blank (1995) reports that unemployment rates for both male and female high school dropouts are almost five times as high as those for college graduates and almost double those of high school graduates, with overall unemployment rates of females just below those of males. Danziger (1989) reports that poor female heads of households who do not receive AFDC still work only twenty-six weeks a year on average, while Moffitt (1992) estimates that AFDC recipients would probably work only fourteen weeks a year if they were not on AFDC. Their employment and labor force participation rates are apparently limited by other problems, such as child care needs and/or personal disabilities (Maynard 1995).

[29] See Holzer (1994b) for a broader discussion of the labor supply versus labor demand issues in interpreting black unemployment problems. In an earlier paper (Holzer, 1986), I argue that relatively high reservation (or minimally acceptable) wages for young blacks might explain some fraction of their higher nonemployment durations than young whites, though this fraction always remained well under half (30–40 percent).

[30] The nonemployment rates of minorities and young workers are even more responsive to the business cycle than are those of older workers or whites. See Clark and Summers (1981), and Freeman (1991).

even lower market wages than exist today.[31] Indeed, the U.S. labor market has been able to absorb many millions of new labor force entrants in the past few decades, many of them young women and/or less-educated immigrants, without significant increases in the overall unemployment rate (though immigrants may well have contributed to the very substantial recent decline in average wages among less-educated workers).[32] For at least some current AFDC recipients, the ultimate problem may well be very low wages and/or high turnover on existing jobs, rather than long-term nonemployment per se.[33]

On the other hand, the adjustment process by which the quantity of labor demanded (the number of available jobs) adjusts to shifts in labor supply can take many years, especially given rigidities in the wage structure. More important, even when this adjustment is completed, very significant long-term nonemployment may continue to be experienced by those groups who are at the "end of the queue" in terms of employer preferences when they are hiring. This has been the case so far for many inner-city minorities and other less-skilled workers, and it will likely be the case for many long-term AFDC recipients in the coming years.[34]

CONCLUSIONS

As we have seen, the vast majority of jobs for non-college graduates require daily use of at least some major cognitive skills, such as reading/writing paragraphs, doing arithmetic, or using com-

[31] Minimum wages and other sources of wage rigidity on the demand side of the labor market may impede the economy's ability to create employment for all of these jobseekers, even in the long run.

[32] See Borjas *et al.* (1992), and Borjas and Ramey (1994) for evidence that immigration of less-skilled workers has reduced demand for native-born workers. Earlier papers (see Card 1990; Lalonde and Topel 1988) came to the opposite conclusion, though these cross-sectional papers may have been plagued by the endogeneity of immigrant locations.

[33] These arguments are summarized in Blank (1995) and Burtless (1995). I will present some data and a discussion of the effects of skill needs on the hiring of minorities (including Hispanics and immigrants) and women in chapter 4, while the wages of these jobs will be considered in chapter 5.

[34] A similar conclusion on the employment prospects of AFDC recipients is reached in Newman and Lennon (1995) based on their research on people who work or seek work at McDonald's establishments in Harlem.

puters. Many of these jobs are filled through referrals from current employees or other sources, especially in blue-collar work.

Most employers require not only high school diplomas and general work experience in filling these jobs, but also specific experience, references, and/or previous training. Many use tests as additional screening tools, and most also require that prospective applicants be interviewed. A strong reluctance on the part of employers to hire those with unstable work histories or criminal records (often suspected rather than confirmed), along with a reliance on referrals from current employees and acquaintances, decreases job prospects even further for those with limited skills and experience.

Overall, only 5–10 percent of the jobs in central-city areas for non-college graduates require very few cognitive skills or work credentials. In these same areas, it appears that a much larger percentage of residents lack at least one or more of the credentials required by employers. Prospective additions to this labor force under welfare reform proposals are likely to be substantial.

Thus, it seems highly probable that the imbalance between job availability and the number of people with low skills and credentials that already exists in many central-city areas will worsen over the next few years.

4 / Who Gets Hired for These Jobs?

Some firms hire more minority or female workers than others do. There are many possible reasons why this is so. Obviously, the kinds of jobs that are available vary across firms, as do their skill requirements. The methods used by employers to meet their need for workers with particular skills may have an effect on who gets hired. And certain characteristics of firms, such as their geographic location within the metropolitan area and their proximity to black populations, as well as the racial attitudes of employers, may also have significant effects with respect to who gets hired.

In this chapter, we will look at how employer recruiting and screening behavior, as well as such characteristics of firms as their location, is related to the characteristics of the people hired into positions that do not require a college degree. We will focus on the *gender* and *race* of newly hired workers. This should give us some insight into the barriers that limit the employment opportunities for minorities, women, and less-skilled workers.

First, we present data on the race and gender of new hires by location of the firm and by industry and occupation. We also consider some other characteristics of these new hires, such as age and education. Then we present data on the race and gender of newly hired workers relative to the skill requirements of jobs and the screens used by employers. By comparing the rates at which minorities and women are hired into jobs that do and do not have specific skill needs, hiring screens, and the like, we will have a better idea of the specific barriers they face.

Of course, the distribution of people across jobs does not only reflect employer choices and preferences; indeed, it is a product of a *matching* process in which people choose the firms and jobs for which they apply and employers decide which applicants they will hire. To more fully understand the characteristics of people that do get hired, we examined each of these two separate processes. We analyzed the *application rates* of minorities to various firms, as well as the ratios of hires (or employees) to these applications. The former is a measure of labor *supply* to various kinds of firms, while the latter is a measure of *demand* for these applicants by these firms. We looked at how both factors affect the distribution of minorities, especially black males and females, across occupations, industries, and geographic areas.

Last, we present the results of logistic (or logit) regression equations in which the probabilities that recently hired workers are in particular race-by-gender groups (for example, white males, black males, etc.) are estimated as functions of firm and job characteristics. These equations enable us to consider the effects of all of these factors simultaneously, while controlling for differences in some of the personal characteristics of the workers themselves (such as their age and education levels). Although the equations are based on data that are strictly cross-sectional in nature (that is, different firms observed at a single point in time), they do have implications for how labor demand has shifted over time in favor of workers with particular labor market skills.

EMPLOYEE CHARACTERISTICS BY LOCATION

It is well known that the residences of blacks in the United States are relatively concentrated in central-city areas, while the residences of whites are more concentrated in suburban areas. Even within these broad (and somewhat arbitrary) categories, significant residential segregation by race exists as well.[1]

[1] The extent and consequences of racial segregation are best summarized in Massey and Denton (1992).

Given the unequal racial distribution of residences, and the fact that commuting within metropolitan areas is not costless, we would expect the racial distribution of workplaces to be unequal as well, with higher percentages of blacks than whites working in central-city areas. Such differences in workplace distribution might imply a "spatial mismatch" limiting the overall wage and employment opportunities of blacks.

The data in table 4.1 reveal that whites are relatively more likely to work in suburban areas and blacks in the central cities, while the workers in the "other" areas are more mixed. There is, of course, some variation in the extent to which this is true across specific groups and/or geographic areas. For instance, the hiring of white males is generally more concentrated in suburban areas than is that of white females; this may well reflect the greater concentration of clerical jobs in the central city that we found above.

The racial gaps in employment between the central cities and the suburbs are most severe in Detroit and least severe in Los Angeles. Thus, the percentage of employees in the Detroit metropolitan area who are black is almost four times as high in the primary central city as in the suburbs; the percentage is twice as high in Boston (at least for males), while in Los Angeles it is roughly the same.

Unlike in the other metropolitan areas, employment for white females in Detroit is even more concentrated in the suburbs than it is for males. One possible (and speculative) interpretation is that this indicates a particularly strong aversion among females to commuting into the central city. There also appears to be a distinct underrepresentation of black males relative to black females among the new hires in Detroit that is not seen elsewhere.[2]

To a large extent, these differences in employment locations for blacks and whites across metropolitan areas parallel the racial segregation of residences and the sharpness of central-city/suburban distinctions more generally (as discussed in chapter 1). On

[2] The relative underrepresentation of black males among new hires could simply reflect a higher tendency for females to be in these high turnover positions, as appears to be the case among whites. But it is not clear why this should only be true in Detroit for blacks. Furthermore, data on overall employment in these firms confirm that there are fewer black males than black females working in them.

Table 4.1 / Race, Gender, and Other Characteristics of New Hires

	Atlanta			Boston		
	PCC[a]	SUB[b]	OTH[c]	PCC	SUB	OTH
Males						
White	.204	.301	.333	.281	.467	.278
Black	.182	.108	.156	.073	.030	.021
Hispanic	.007	.024	.012	.026	.026	.257
Asian	.019	.003	.013	.004	.028	.006
Females						
White	.378	.433	.279	.455	.403	.302
Black	.170	.108	.174	.071	.010	.054
Hispanic	.028	.006	.014	.075	.022	.077
Asian	.003	.018	.000	.014	.013	.005
Education						
College Graduate	.437	.252	.323	.367	.407	.440
Some College	.186	.224	.144	.263	.161	.129
High School Graduate	.355	.437	.500	.355	.384	.358
High School Dropout	.022	.087	.033	.016	.047	.073
Age						
16–24	.246	.237	.218	.190	.249	.337
25–34	.439	.332	.476	.456	.355	.325
35+	.315	.430	.306	.354	.395	.339

NOTE. The numbers in this table sum approximately to one *vertically* within each of the three categories of race/gender, education, and age.
[a] Primary central city.
[b] Suburbs.
[c] Other areas, as defined in table 2.2.

the other hand, the lower tendency for white females to work in the city of Detroit than in other central cities, and the apparently lower tendency for black males to work there at all, together suggest that a variety of factors other than residential segregation (higher levels of racial tension, poverty, and crime, which may themselves be functions of residential segregation) may also be relevant there.

When we compare blacks and other minority groups in terms of geographic concentration of employment, we discover that there does not seem to be any consistent tendency for Hispanic and Asian employment to be concentrated in the central cities (though sample sizes in the metropolitan areas other than Los Angeles for these groups are small). In Los Angeles, we find em-

	Detroit			Los Angeles		
	PCC	SUB	OTH	PCC	SUB	OTH
Males						
White	.223	.387	.264	.086	.160	.150
Black	.193	.055	.140	.048	.049	.173
Hispanic	.007	.017	.016	.291	.192	.164
Asian	.002	.002	.029	.146	.033	.038
Females						
White	.250	.436	.363	.169	.277	.191
Black	.292	.086	.162	.053	.049	.033
Hispanic	.025	.006	.019	.152	.171	.158
Asian	.000	.007	.000	.041	.058	.094
Education						
College Graduate	.286	.239	.221	.362	.246	.543
Some College	.213	.332	.409	.217	.257	.173
High School Graduate	.446	.386	.339	.346	.445	.253
High School Dropout	.055	.043	.031	.075	.052	.032
Age						
16–24	.252	.304	.299	.224	.238	.153
25–34	.340	.330	.272	.408	.364	.589
35+	.409	.367	.430	.368	.398	.258

ployment for Hispanic and Asian males—but not for females—relatively concentrated in the central city (more than is true for blacks). The reason for this pattern is not clear.

Workers with college degrees and young adult workers (ages 25–34) are considerably more likely to work in the central city than are others; apparently, these groups are more willing than others to live in or commute to the center city. Again, Detroit is the exception. Employment in the Detroit central city declines monotonically with age; thus, young adults seem more reluctant to commute into the central city there than elsewhere.[3]

We present data in table C.1 in appendix C on the distributions of employment by race and gender for central cities and suburbs within each of the four metropolitan areas among those in jobs

[3]When the data on job requirements from chapter 3 are computed separately for jobs that hired younger (age 34 or less) versus older workers, the results appear very similar across the two groups. Skill requirements and hiring criteria for the former averaged just a few percentage points below those observed for the latter.

requiring no college or those with high school degrees or less, first for all age groups combined and then for those aged 16–34 only. The distributions in this table look fairly similar to those in table 4.1. Comparing the data in the two tables, we generally find that the racial gaps in the location of employment are somewhat greater among less-educated workers and jobs but somewhat smaller for the young. The smaller racial gaps among the young indicate a greater degree of job suburbanization among younger blacks than older ones, though the overall racial patterns by location remain fairly strong even for younger blacks.

Overall, this demonstrated tendency for employment to be relatively concentrated in the primary central cities for blacks and in the suburbs for whites is certainly consistent with the notion of "spatial mismatch." This hypothesis posits that the employment and wage opportunities of blacks are limited by the residential segregation of blacks in inner-city areas as well as by difficulties in obtaining transportation and information, which lower their access to the job market that is growing more suburbanized.

These data do not prove spatial mismatch. It is at least possible that there could be enough jobs in the central city with limited skill requirements to employ all of the residents there who wanted work, and at comparable wages to what they might earn elsewhere. But from the evidence in the previous chapters, which indicates a higher demand for skills in central-city jobs (even those that do not require a college degree) than in suburban ones as well as a higher ratio of unemployed workers to vacant jobs in the central cities, this possibility does not appear likely.

EMPLOYEE CHARACTERISTICS BY OCCUPATION, INDUSTRY, AND LOCATION

Occupational segregation by race and by gender has been explored at length by economists. The distributions of these groups across occupations may be the result of decisions made by workers or employers. Employers may choose differently among applicants of diverse race or gender groups because of real differences in skills or because of discriminatory perceptions of their abilities.[4]

[4] Different interpretations of occupational segregation by gender can be found in Killingsworth (1990) and Sorensen (1994). Occupational segregation by race was dis-

The distributions of workers across industries by race and gender may also be due partly to the occupational makeup of these industries and partly to independent factors.

The distributions illustrated in table 4.2 are *across* occupations or industries, the data from our survey having been computed separately for each of six race-by-gender groups. Again, we limit our sample to jobs that do not require college degrees.

Almost half of the females recently hired into non-college jobs work in clerical jobs, while another 30 percent work in professional/managerial and sales positions. Black women are somewhat underrepresented in these white-collar positions (except for sales) and more heavily represented in service jobs. Hispanic women are less represented in the professional/managerial and sales jobs and somewhat more concentrated in blue-collar positions.

Even among males in non-college positions, about 40 percent now work in blue-collar jobs, while the remaining 60 percent are employed in white-collar or service jobs. By race, we find that relative to white males, black males are underrepresented in white-collar jobs (except clerical jobs) and in skilled blue-collar positions (that is, in the crafts), while being heavily overrepresented in service jobs. In contrast, Hispanic males are the most heavily represented of all groups in blue-collar jobs. Likewise, black males are underrepresented in manufacturing jobs, while Hispanics are heavily overrepresented. In fact, among blacks, newly hired females are now as likely to work in manufacturing as are males; this is not true for either of the other racial groups.

This striking underrepresentation of black males in manufacturing, and their growing presence in service jobs and industries, is a relatively new phenomenon.[5] It parallels the concentration of manufacturing in the suburbs and services in the central cities that we noted in chapter 2. Residential patterns may also account for the relatively greater success that Hispanics have in obtaining

cussed in Becker's classic work on discrimination (1971) and also in Bergmann (1971), with more recent evidence appearing in Hirsch and MacPherson (1994).

[5]As of 1970, black males were as concentrated in manufacturing as white males nationwide and significantly more so in the Midwest (Bound and Holzer 1993). Over the next two decades, black male employment in manufacturing deteriorated much more substantially than did that of any other race/gender group, especially in the Midwest (Bound and Holzer 1995).

Table 4.2 / Occupations and Industries of New Hires into Non-College Jobs by Race and Gender

	Occupation						
	Prof/Mgt.	Sales	Clerical	Craft	Operative	Laborer	Service
Males							
White	.143	.173	.128	.185	.175	.067	.121
Black	.063	.138	.153	.095	.209	.097	.238
Hispanic	.078	.078	.137	.167	.280	.113	.144
Females							
White	.194	.155	.488	.016	.037	.006	.097
Black	.111	.180	.429	.030	.052	.014	.183
Hispanic	.075	.112	.489	.029	.141	.023	.130

	Industry							
	Constr.	Mfg.	TCU	W. Trade	R. Trade	Fire	Service	Public
Males								
White	.041	.291	.058	.111	.179	.062	.245	.013
Black	.026	.199	.131	.075	.214	.023	.308	.025
Hispanic	.018	.448	.035	.074	.126	.034	.244	.021
Females								
White	.019	.157	.045	.067	.172	.145	.386	.010
Black	.000	.194	.055	.041	.239	.122	.398	.027
Hispanic	.007	.211	.024	.035	.163	.091	.457	.013

NOTE: The numbers sum to approximately one horizontally.

the traditional blue-collar jobs, since they are not as segregated residentially as blacks.

On the other hand, it is doubtful that differences in residential locations between the two minority groups are large enough to fully account for this trend. Furthermore, the relatively greater presence of black females in these blue-collar jobs (relative to white and Hispanic females) makes the spatial mismatch hypothesis less compelling as the single explanation for this trend, since black women are no less likely to be residentially segregated than black males and have limited access to suburbanizing jobs.

We present more detailed data on the interactions between occupation/industry, geographic area, and race/gender in appendix C. The distributions of each of the six race-by-gender groups are shown across occupations or industries separately for each metropolitan area in table C.2. The occupations we present fall into four broad categories: professional/managerial, sales/clerical, craft/operative, and laborer/service; the industries we present fall into three categories: manufacturing, retail trade, and services.

The data show that certain employment patterns across groups are common to all four of the metropolitan areas. For instance, black males are slightly underrepresented in the craft/operative category and overrepresented in the laborer/service category relative to white males in each of the four metropolitan areas and relative to Hispanics in all but one. They are also underrepresented in manufacturing relative to Hispanics in all areas and to whites in all but one.[6] Among females, the relatively greater concentration of blacks in laborer/service work and their relative underrepresentation in professional/managerial jobs is also true virtually everywhere.

Data on the distribution of workers in non-college jobs across race-gender groups for certain specific occupational or industrial groupings (sales/clerical jobs, craft/operative jobs, manufacturing, and services) are presented for central-city and suburban areas within each metropolitan area in table C.3.[7] This enables

[6] Only in Atlanta is the presence of black males in manufacturing comparable to that of white males.

[7] Unlike the data in tables 4.2 or C.2, the data in this table present race/gender distributions for jobs within specific occupational or industrial groups, rather than the occupational distribution for specific race/gender groups.

us to see whether some of the racial employment patterns we observed exist *within* the central cities and suburbs of each metropolitan area as well as *between* them, since residential segregation factors should account for the latter but not the former.

Broadly speaking, the data reveal that the underrepresentation of blacks in manufacturing employment among males is generally much larger in the suburbs than in the central cities; in Los Angeles and Boston, however, black males have virtually no representation in manufacturing jobs even in the central cities, while in the Atlanta central city almost as many of these jobs are filled by whites as by blacks.

Likewise, the fractions of craft/operative jobs going to white males are many times higher than those going to black males in each suburban area; in the central cities the black presence in these jobs is more substantial but blacks predominate only in Atlanta.[8] The high percentages of Hispanic males (and also females) in blue-collar and manufacturing employment in Los Angeles occur in both the central city and in the suburbs.

These data strongly imply that residential segregation factors constitute just one of many potential determinants of the pattern of racial and gender hiring that we have observed. To better understand the other determinants, we need to look at how other job characteristics, employer hiring behavior, and employee search patterns affect the tendency for various groups to be employed in different kinds of jobs.

RACE AND GENDER EFFECTS OF SKILL REQUIREMENTS AND HIRING SCREENS

To what extent can the distributions of workers by race and gender across occupations, industries, and locations be explained by the skill requirements of jobs and the hiring behavior of employers? To answer this question, we compare the distributions of new

[8] White males are hired for 53 percent of such jobs in the central city of Detroit and black males for 31 percent, even though white males account for 20 percent and black males 22 percent of all recent hires there.

Table 4.3 / Race and Gender of New Hires for Non-College Jobs by Daily Task Use

	White Males	Black Males	Hispanic Males	White Females	Black Females	Hispanic Females
All Jobs	.260	.096	.089	.341	.102	.067
Talking to Customers						
Yes	.232	.081	.057	.412	.114	.066
No	.327	.130	.163	.176	.076	.065
Reading/Writing						
Yes	.260	.086	.073	.363	.098	.068
No	.260	.110	.114	.305	.109	.065
Arithmetic						
Yes	.283	.079	.072	.374	.090	.057
No	.217	.128	.121	.281	.124	.085
Computers						
Yes	.193	.064	.039	.465	.117	.071
No	.326	.128	.140	.215	.087	.062

NOTE: The top line of this table shows the distribution of employees across *all* jobs; the subsequent lines show the distribution of employees by race and gender in jobs in which each of the tasks is or is not required. The numbers sum approximately to one horizontally.

employees by race and gender in jobs that have the particular skill requirements, hiring screens, and so on that we examined in the previous chapter with those that do not have them. We do this only for jobs that do not require college degrees, so that differences in educational attainments between whites, blacks, and Hispanics are at least partly controlled for.

Our survey yielded results that show clear patterns by both race and gender for each of the tasks—talking to customers, reading/writing paragraphs, doing arithmetic, and using computers—considered. As we can see from the data in table 4.3, within virtually every racial or ethnic group, females are more likely than males to be found in jobs that require the performance of these tasks. This is especially true for jobs in which employees must talk to customers and use computers daily. The predominance of female employment in jobs with these task requirements is at least partly due to their concentration in clerical, sales, and service occupations, where the daily use of these tasks is relatively high.

However, there are also clear patterns here by racial/ethnic group. Within each gender, whites are more likely than blacks and Hispanics to be found in jobs requiring any of these tasks. Thus, even though white males are not highly concentrated in these jobs relative to white females (except, to some extent, in jobs that use arithmetic), they are much more likely to be found in each of these job categories relative to black or Hispanic males; and, given the gender effect, black and Hispanic females are also more likely to be found in these jobs than are their male counterparts.

The underrepresentation of black and Hispanic males is most evident in jobs using computers and is even more severe for Hispanics than for blacks. A strong underrepresentation of black and Hispanic males relative to whites of either sex is also seen in jobs requiring reading/writing and arithmetic.

It is important to remember that the list of tasks and skills that we considered is not exhaustive; a different list of tasks (especially those requiring physical strength or managerial responsibilities) would likely have generated a different pattern of employment by both gender and race.

However, the cognitive/interactive skills we considered appear to be the ones for which labor demand has been growing in recent years, especially among the less educated. Indeed, these results imply an increase in labor demand in recent years for females relative to males and for whites relative to blacks and Hispanics, which is consistent with the wage and employment trends for these groups in the 1980s.[9]

On the other hand, they also imply that the employment prospects for less-educated females, particularly minorities, without strong cognitive/interactive skills may be seriously limited as well. Since many of the *longer-term* AFDC recipients who will now be required to seek employment likely fit this profile (see chapter 3), their ability to quickly gain and retain employment (even at low wages) must be regarded as questionable at best.

It is possible that blacks and Hispanics are underrepresented

[9]See Blau and Kahn (1994) and Bound and Holzer (1995) for evidence on wage gains during the 1980s by less-educated females relative to males and less-educated whites relative to blacks within each gender. These results are also fully consistent with those of O'Neill (1990), Ferguson (1993), Neal and Johnson (1994), and others who have found relatively strong effects of Armed Forces Qualifying Test scores on the relative earnings and employment of blacks and whites.

in jobs requiring certain skills (like computer use) because of discriminatory employers who underestimate their abilities, rather than because of their skill deficiencies per se. Indeed, if the skills used in these jobs are acquired through on-the-job training, hiring decisions may in fact determine who acquires these skills in the first place.[10]

The race and gender patterns observed across the categories of jobs with different skill requirements raise questions about how hiring activities and attitudes among employers may generate these outcomes. It has long been alleged that certain recruiting and screening methods disproportionately keep female and/or minority job applicants from being hired. Indeed, screens that create "disparate impacts" on hiring across groups, and that may or may not be related to actual job performance, have generated a significant legal and legislative response, as well as attempts by some firms to "validate" their hiring criteria by linking them to actual job performance.[11]

When we look at race and gender outcomes for non-college jobs that require particular credentials (high school diplomas, general or specific experience, previous training), or in which certain screens (tests, education or criminal record checks, and interviews) are used, or in which affirmative action plays a role in recruiting and screening versus jobs that do not require credentials or employ screens or affirmative action, we find a similar pattern by race and gender to that for tasks. As the data in table 4.4 illustrate, within most racial groups, females are more likely than males to be found in jobs requiring a high school diploma or general experience, as well as those in which tests (other than

[10]Bishop (1993) argues that employers have relatively little information about an applicant's prospective productivity when they make hiring decisions and therefore that productivity "surprises" are frequent. Under these circumstances there is considerable room for discriminatory judgments about who will be competent in performing a variety of job-specific tasks.

[11]In *Griggs v. Duke Power* (1971), the Supreme Court put the burden of proof on the employer to demonstrate a statistical link between hiring screens and actual job performance when the former had "disparate impacts" on the hiring of minorities. This decision was partially overturned in *Ward Cove v. Atonio* (1989) and then largely restored through the Civil Rights Act of 1991. Of course, firms that successfully validate their screens may continue to use them despite their "disparate impacts," and firms that have faced no litigation on this issue (and have few concerns about prospective litigation) may use such screens without having them validated.

Table 4.4 / Race and Gender of New Hires for Non-College Jobs by Use of Hiring Screens

	White Males	Black Males	Hispanic Males	White Females	Black Females	Hispanic Females
Requirements for Hiring						
High School Diploma						
Yes	.251	.081	.055	.396	.106	.064
No	.281	.132	.174	.200	.094	.075
General Experience						
Yes	.266	.083	.078	.368	.096	.066
No	.244	.124	.114	.281	.117	.069
Specific Experience						
Yes	.268	.079	.079	.356	.094	.071
No	.246	.121	.104	.317	.116	.060
References						
Yes	.264	.094	.085	.355	.101	.065
No	.249	.099	.101	.303	.104	.072
Other Training						
Yes	.287	.079	.087	.347	.083	.069
No	.243	.107	.091	.336	.115	.065
Other Screens						
Test/Physical						
Yes	.220	.149	.102	.254	.114	.082
No	.268	.085	.086	.358	.100	.064
Test/Other						
Yes	.219	.087	.091	.361	.113	.075
No	.264	.099	.087	.338	.102	.064
Check Education						
Yes	.234	.099	.069	.353	.117	.088
No	.271	.096	.097	.335	.094	.059
Check for Criminal Record						
Yes	.241	.116	.075	.318	.129	.072
No	.267	.087	.096	.351	.091	.067
Interview						
Yes	.255	.093	.084	.358	.099	.068
No	.288	.119	.126	.273	.127	.059
Use Affirmative Action						
Yes	.217	.098	.092	.358	.112	.074
No	.314	.093	.085	.318	.090	.058

NOTE: Numbers sum to approximately one horizontally.

physicals) and interviews are given. Gender patterns in jobs using other screens are somewhat less clear-cut, and males are more likely than females to appear in a few categories (such as jobs that require physical tests and, among whites, those that require previous training).

In contrast, patterns by race within each gender group remain very strong. Black and Hispanic males are particularly underrepresented relative to whites in all jobs requiring credentials. Black males are especially underrepresented in jobs requiring specific experience, while Hispanic males are most underrepresented in jobs requiring high school diplomas.[12]

The importance of prior work experience for blacks suggests that many may be "scarred" by unemployment early on. The early literature on this subject questioned the notion that early unemployment causes later unemployment, but recent evidence is somewhat more supportive of this idea.[13] Our findings underline the importance of improving the "school-to-work" transition for young blacks.

Black and Hispanic males are more likely than other groups to be found where physical tests are given and where background checks are performed by employers. It is not likely, however, that screens per se have a positive effect on their employment, rather that blacks and Hispanics are less likely to apply for jobs that do not have such screens.

Affirmative action appears to have small positive effects on the employment of each race-by-gender group except for white males, for whom the effects appear to be strongly negative. This suggests that these programs may be redistributing employment opportunities from the latter to the former, as intended.

When we look at the race and gender composition of jobs for which employers say that they either would or would not hire individuals with a stigmatizing characteristic, or do or do not regard any of a set of personal characteristics to be important in an interview situation, we see clear relationships (illustrated in table 4.5) between employer attitudes and the race and gender of employees hired. In particular, employers who say that they would hire welfare recipients are in fact more likely to hire black females; those who say they would hire applicants with unstable work

[12] This last finding is consistent with the high dropout rate from high school among Hispanics relative to both whites and blacks. See Hauser and Phang (1993).

[13] For instance, Ellwood (1982), and Meyer and Wise (1982) both find little evidence of longer-term *employment* effects from early unemployment but some evidence of *wage* effects. But Hotz and Tienda (1994) find evidence that the lack of employment among minority high school students reduces future employment, while Rich (1994) suggests that these effects might exist for youth more generally.

Table 4.5 / Race and Gender of New Hires for Non-College Jobs by Employer Attitudes and Preferences

	White Males	Black Males	Hispanic Males	White Females	Black Females	Hispanic Females
Would Hire						
Welfare Recipient						
Yes	.250	.094	.091	.344	.110	.065
No	.313	.104	.079	.321	.061	.074
GED/Government Trainee						
Yes	.253	.097	.096	.355	.102	.069
No	.291	.088	.058	.366	.102	.056
Only Part-Time or Short-Term Experience						
Yes	.240	.097	.084	.342	.106	.085
No	.278	.094	.094	.340	.099	.049
Unemployment of at Least One Year						
Yes	.246	.089	.096	.343	.101	.074
No	.290	.110	.074	.336	.105	.050
Criminal Record						
Yes	.271	.111	.103	.316	.083	.058
No	.254	.088	.082	.353	.112	.071
Important Interview Factors						
Physical Appearance/ Neatness						
Yes	.222	.088	.068	.382	.123	.070
No	.296	.107	.111	.298	.080	.063
English/Verbal Skills						
Yes	.231	.086	.056	.405	.110	.069
No	.318	.124	.166	.192	.086	.062
Politeness						
Yes	.236	.085	.074	.386	.107	.065
No	.328	.139	.138	.194	.089	.071
Motivation						
Yes	.265	.088	.081	.358	.098	.062
No	.235	.123	.109	.299	.117	.079

NOTE: Numbers sum to approximately one horizontally.

histories are more likely to hire both black and Hispanic females; and those who say they would hire applicants with criminal records are more likely to hire black and Hispanic males.[14]

[14]The last effect is also observable for white males, though its relative magnitude is a good deal smaller than for blacks and Hispanics.

In interviews, physical appearance and neatness matter more for jobs in which females are likely to be hired, as do English/verbal skills and politeness. Hispanic males are particularly underrepresented in jobs where English/verbal skills matter, and black males and females are least likely to be hired (relative to other ethnic groups within their gender) for jobs requiring a demonstration of motivation.

Thus, despite the subjectivity of employer attitude and preference questions, and our concerns about the extent to which the responses to our questions reflect actual employer behavior, we find that there are relationships between the tasks and hiring behavior/attitudes we considered and who actually gets hired. The extent to which these relationships are still observed after we control for a variety of other firm and job characteristics will be explored below.

With respect to the race and gender compositions of new hires in jobs involving few or no tasks and hiring requirements, the results of our survey clearly show that black and Hispanic males are much more likely to be employed in jobs requiring few or no tasks and hiring requirements. In fact, as the data in table 4.6 reveal, black males are almost twice as likely to be employed in jobs that require no daily task performance as in those that require the performance of at least some tasks; for Hispanic males the ratio is roughly three to one. The required performance of daily tasks and the requirement for a high school diploma have the largest negative effects on the hiring of Hispanic males, while experience and previous training requirements have relatively larger negative effects on the hiring of black males. Furthermore, these patterns appear to exist in jobs located in both the central cities and suburban areas, with no consistent pattern of larger differentials in one location or the other.[15]

When we compare black and Hispanic females to white females, we find similar results. For instance, the ratio of black female to white female hires in jobs requiring no daily tasks is roughly six to ten; in those jobs requiring at least one daily task, this ratio drops by roughly half to about three to ten.

The hiring of minorities is significantly lower for jobs that require the daily performance of cognitive/social tasks and for which

[15] These results are available from the author.

Table 4.6 / Race and Gender of New Hires for Non-College Jobs for Jobs with Few Tasks and Little Screening

	White Males	Black Males	Hispanic Males	White Females	Black Females	Hispanic Females
Perform None of Major Tasks Daily						
Yes	.291	.165	.239	.104	.061	.092
No	.257	.090	.076	.362	.106	.064
Perform None of Tasks Except Talking to Customers						
Yes	.280	.146	.187	.182	.085	.084
No	.256	.088	.074	.365	.105	.064
Requires No High School Diploma, Training, Experience, or References						
Yes	.229	.189	.152	.179	.116	.066
No	.261	.090	.085	.350	.102	.067
Requires Only High School Diploma						
Yes	.257	.172	.118	.214	.121	.073
No	.260	.089	.086	.352	.101	.066
Requires Only High School Diploma and General Experience						
Yes	.241	.152	.115	.254	.136	.067
No	.262	.089	.086	.352	.098	.067

NOTE: Numbers sum to approximately one horizontally.

hiring screens are not insignificant. This is true even for jobs that do not require college degrees. For subgroups of the workforce that are particularly lacking in skills and credentials (such as high school dropouts, long-term AFDC recipients, and males with criminal records), the implications of these results for their employment prospects are especially grim.

APPLICANT VERSUS HIRE RATES

The distributions of various groups of workers across job categories depend not only on the hiring choices of employers but are also affected by worker choices about where to apply for jobs. They are the outcome of a *matching* process between the demand

and supply sides of the labor market, in which workers search for the jobs for which they apply and employers then choose among applicants.

The literature on the job-search choices of workers (and, to a lesser extent, on employers' choices) is voluminous, and we will not attempt to summarize it here.[16] For our purposes, we assumed that worker choices on where to apply depend on the location of the job (relative to where the worker lives); the wages and benefits of the job (relative to the worker's own reservation wages and benefits, which are the minimum that they consider acceptable); other attributes of the job and the work involved (relative to the worker's own preferences with respect to such attributes); and the requirements of the job, in terms of the skills or other personal characteristics required (relative to the worker's own).

The last of these factors is partly dependent on the worker's subjective perceptions of what employers seek when hiring people. Presumably, workers will not apply for jobs in which they think there is a very low chance of being hired, unless it is virtually costless for them to do so and/or the returns to being hired (in terms of wages and benefits) are very high.

Workers are also more likely to apply for jobs in firms where they have a personal contact, usually a friend or relative who might be employed at the firm or who is an acquaintance of the employer. Such contacts are important conduits of information to applicants about the nature and availability of jobs, as well as the source of recommendations and referrals to employers (which, as we know from the previous chapter, many employers actively seek).[17]

Thus, black workers are more likely to search and apply for jobs that are located in the central city, where many of them live, and in occupations and industries where they have frequently been hired in relatively large numbers, about which they may have information and contacts, and where they think they will be

[16] See Davidson (1990) for a review of theoretical models and Devine and Kiefer (1991) for a review of empirical evidence.

[17] For more evidence on the importance of friends and relatives in the search process for employees, see Rees (1966), Granovetter (1974), Corcoran, Datcher, and Duncan (1980), and Holzer (1988). For more theoretical models of the importance of social networks on employment outcomes, see Montgomery (1991).

welcome.[18] This probably holds true for Hispanics and females as well.

Employers must choose among applicants on the basis of the skills and personal characteristics they perceive them to possess, relative to the minimum (or *reservation*) requirements of the jobs they are trying to fill. Their choices then determine who gets hired into which jobs and the resulting employment and wage rates for different groups of workers.[19]

Of course, employer perceptions and preferences may be discriminatory by race and/or gender, and the degree of discrimination may well vary by the employer's location or by the occupation or industry for which he or she is hiring.[20] In any event, the recruitment and screening procedures that employers use will generally be the mechanisms through which these perceptions of workers are formed and these preferences exercised.

In our survey, we asked employers what percentages of their applicants were black males, black females, Hispanics, and Asians. We then calculated the percentages of non-college employees at each firm and the percentages of the firm's new hires who are members of each group. The ratios of the means of each of these measures to the means of the applicant measures for each group are presented in table 4.7.[21]

[18] For more evidence on the search choices of black workers, see Holzer (1986, 1987b), Holzer, Ihlanfeldt, and Sjoquist (1994), and Farley, Holzer, and Danziger (1995).

[19] At least in the short term, we assume that the characteristics of jobs are fixed and that employers must find workers who meet certain requirements that are at least minimally necessary. Wages of such jobs are likely to be fixed in the short term as well. In the longer term, both job characteristics and wages will adjust to changes in technology, the characteristics of the workforce, and the like. For models of employer search, see Barron, Berger, and Black (1994) and Barron, Bishop, and Dunkelberg (1985).

[20] Employer discrimination may be *statistical*, if employers perceive lower *average* qualifications among particular groups (such as minorities or women) and if they use these group averages to judge *individual* job applicants within these groups (Cain 1986). On the other hand, discrimination may be *pure* if it is based strictly on employers' preferences or on those of their employees and customers (Becker 1971). If employers perceive a certain group's qualifications or skills to be lower than they are in reality, we can consider this a combination of pure and statistical discrimination.

[21] There are advantages and disadvantages with each measure of employment for the group in question. The fraction of the firm's employees is based on a firm-wide measure, as is the application measure, while the fraction of new hires is occupation-specific. On the other hand, the latter will be more representative of recent hiring than the former. The firm-wide variables also appear to have some measurement error at the firm level, while the most recent hire for each firm may contain more random "noise."

Table 4.7 / Applicant and Hire Rates

	Primary Central City	Suburbs	Other Areas[a]
Percent of Applicants Who Are			
Black Males	.229	.119	.186
Black Females	.189	.093	.145
Hispanics	.151	.137	.130
Asians	.057	.058	.047
Ratio of Employees to Applicants For			
Black Males	.642	.555	.640
Black Females	.926	.581	.751
Hispanics	.974	.993	.731
Asians	.905	.759	.548
Ratio of New Hires to Applicants For			
Black Males	.620	.496	.640
Black Females	.836	.699	.786
Hispanics	1.000	1.022	1.223
Asians	.930	.690	.596

[a] As defined in table 2.2.

Differences in the applicant rates across locations can be interpreted as differences in the quantity of labor *supply* from each group, while differences in the ratios of employees or hires to applicants are measures of differences in *demand* for the applicants of that group (whether due to skill imbalances, discrimination, or other factors). Ratios below one for any group indicate, on average, a relative disinclination of employers to hire applicants from that group, while ratios above one indicate a relative preference for applicants from a particular group.[22]

As the data in table 4.7 illustrate, application rates from blacks are roughly twice as high in primary central-city areas as in the suburbs; the ratio of hires (employees) to applicants is roughly one for Hispanics but below one for blacks; the ratio is substantially higher for black females than for black males in all locations; and the ratio is higher for blacks in the primary central-city areas than in the suburbs, with "other" areas somewhere in between.

[22] If all race-gender groups were listed, and if all ratios were measured accurately, the group-weighted sum of ratios should be one.

The higher applicant rate from blacks in the central cities indicates that *access* to jobs for minorities likely depends on the location of employers relative to minority residential areas, which is consistent with the "spatial mismatch" hypothesis. Indeed, the ratio of black *applicants* across the two locations approximates the ratio of black *employment* in these locations (see table 4.1), implying that limited access to suburban jobs for blacks during the application process largely accounts for the relative employment concentrations of blacks and whites by geographic area.

Whether the access of central-city blacks to employment in the suburbs is limited because of transportation difficulties, limited information, weak social contacts, or general perceptions of hostility there is unclear from the data presented here, though there is evidence published elsewhere that lends support to each of these possibilities.[23]

The differences in hiring ratios across racial/ethnic groups, genders, and locations must be interpreted with caution. The hiring ratios across different groups are clearly conditional on the characteristics of those in each applicant pool. Thus, there may be differences across groups in the average *quality* of applicants that are unobservable to us.

Such differences might reflect not only average differences across the relevant populations, but also differences generated by the *self-selection processes* in which workers choose to become applicants to particular employers. For instance, some groups might be more likely than others to apply for lower-wage jobs due to their own lower reservation wages (relative to wage offers), or they might be more likely to apply for jobs at which their chances of being hired are greater, perhaps because they possess better information than others about what particular employers seek.[24]

[23] In Farley, Holzer, and Danziger (1995), we show that applicant rates from blacks vary within the Detroit suburbs according to a variety of factors, such as distance from the central city, the presence of blacks in the residential population, and other factors. Data from the accompanying household survey also indicate that black central-city residents are far more likely to have searched for employment in suburbs that are perceived as being friendly to blacks (in Southfield, for example) as in those perceived to be hostile (Warren, for example), controlling for distance from the central city. The former also have greater residential populations of blacks than the latter, which perhaps provides a source of information and contacts for the central-city residents.

[24] Having referrals from current employees at an establishment may therefore not only influence the employer hiring decision but also the characteristics of the applicants

Either way, some groups will be more appropriately matched to employers than others, with resulting differences in hiring probabilities that do not necessarily reflect demand-side factors. These possibilities must be kept in mind as we consider our findings.

For instance, the higher hiring ratio for Hispanics than for blacks out of all applicants might indicate that Hispanics are more skilled than blacks or that their reservation wages are lower. But, in fact, the Hispanic applicants are much more likely than blacks to be immigrants, with less schooling and weaker interactive skills on average than those of native-born workers; moreover, the levels of educational attainment of all Hispanics (immigrant and nonimmigrant, combined) are generally lower than those of blacks.

While we have no direct evidence on relative reservation wages (the minimum wages considered to be acceptable) for members of these groups, the wages received by Hispanics in our sample are not significantly lower than those of blacks, as we would expect them to be if Hispanics' reservation wages were lower.[25] Nor do the blue-collar or manufacturing jobs in which Hispanics are now heavily concentrated appear to be the types of jobs that blacks would consider unacceptable.

Apparently, *employers prefer Hispanics to blacks* for many jobs in which skill and hiring requirements—especially in terms of formal education and verbal skills—are modest.[26] This finding is consistent with the qualitative evidence on the development of effective social networks for Hispanics in particular industries (Waldinger 1987), and on the general perception by employers that blacks are more troublesome and less compliant employees than the members of many immigrant groups (Kirschenman and Neckerman 1991).[27]

---

who apply. But if employers recruit through their current employees as a way of generating applicants from their preferred groups, the demand-side interpretation of group differences in hiring rates would be valid.

[25] See the data in chapter 5 on the relative wages of blacks and Hispanics who are newly hired. More direct evidence on self-reported reservation wages among blacks and Hispanics will be available in the Boston and Los Angeles household surveys from the Multi-City Study of Urban Inequality.

[26] On the other hand, Hispanics also appear to be preferred to blacks even when experience and previous training are needed.

[27] If Hispanics are willing to apply for and accept low-wage jobs that blacks are not willing to consider, this would also raise their ratio of hires to applicants, even though it would reflect supply-side rather than demand-side preferences.

Whatever the reason, many less-skilled black females, as well as black males, may find themselves behind Hispanics, whether immigrant or native-born, in the queue of workers for available jobs (as determined by employer preferences).[28] Therefore, the apparent availability of jobs for less-educated Hispanic immigrants in recent years does not mean that the same is true for all less-skilled workers, particularly black males and those black females who are long-term AFDC recipients.

Furthermore, Hispanics do not appear to be disadvantaged in access to suburban jobs, as measured by their relative applicant rates in different parts of metropolitan areas. This likely reflects the much lesser racial segregation of Hispanics than blacks in housing (Frey and Farley 1993), and it gives the Hispanics greater access to manufacturing and blue-collar jobs that have clearly become more concentrated in suburban areas.

The apparent preference of employers for black females relative to black males does not appear to be attributable to higher education levels or lower relative reservation wages among the females.[29] In fact, this pattern has also been noted in qualitative employer interviews by Kirschenman (1991), who attributed them to employer fears of crime or violence, and to the greater "attitude" problems that employers perceive among black males.

These findings may also reflect the preponderance of clerical, sales, and service jobs (in which there is a general preference for females) in our sample of newly filled positions. In any event, the magnitudes of these differences in employer preferences between black females and males, which average roughly 20 percentage points, are not insignificant.

Finally, we note the relatively lower *employer preference for black*

[28] These findings do not necessarily imply that there is no discrimination against Hispanic applicants relative to whites. Indeed, audit studies of employer hiring have found some evidence of discrimination against Hispanic applicants (Cross *et al.* 1990; Kenney and Wissoker 1994). While hiring ratios for Hispanics observed here are close to one, the "adding-up constraint" on ratios across groups implies that the ratios are greater than one for whites. Whether all of this relative preference for whites over Hispanics is due to employer skill needs instead of discrimination is not clear from these data.

[29] In Farley, Holzer, and Danziger (1995), we provide some evidence on self-reported reservation wages and received wages by race and gender in Detroit. There is little evidence there of lower relative reservation wages for black females than black males.

applicants in suburban areas than elsewhere. Clearly, the magnitude of this difference across geographic areas is smaller than the difference across areas in *black applicant rates*—in other words, the differences in minority labor supply across areas (which average roughly 100 percent between central city and suburb) are greater than the differences in demand (which average 10–20 percent).

Nevertheless, the differences in demand are large enough to merit concern. Since skill needs and hiring requirements are, on average, greater in the central cities than in the suburbs, and since there is no evidence that the relative gap in skills between black and white applicants is greater in the suburbs,[30] these data strongly suggest that discrimination against blacks is greater among suburban employers than among those located in the central city.[31]

The parallels between the racial applicant and hiring ratio differences across geographic areas (with both being relatively higher for blacks in the central cities) strongly suggest that discriminatory employers may deliberately choose locations for their firms that make them inaccessible to blacks (and to the enforcement of equal employment opportunity (EEO) regulations).[32] In that case, disentangling the "spatial" (location) from the "racial" effects in employment becomes more difficult, and policy approaches that emphasize the former (improved transportation and placement programs) may be ineffective unless they also pay some attention to the latter (perhaps by having the EEO increase its targeting of suburban areas) as well.

When we look at the intrametropolitan differences in the supply of and the demand for minority labor within the four metro-

[30] Data in Hauser and Phang (1993) clearly show that the racial gap in educational attainment is higher in the central cities than in the suburbs. Furthermore, data from the Detroit Area Survey show that highly educated whites are relatively more likely to commute to work in the central city, while their black counterparts are more likely to work in the suburbs (Farley, Holzer, and Danziger 1995).

[31] In both methodology and substance, these results bear some resemblance to those in the audit studies of employers that found discrimination in hiring against blacks (Fix and Struyk 1993; Bendick, Jackson, and Reinoso 1994), since the comparison here controls for both the quantity and the quality of black and white applicants in these two locations. However, the audit studies did not focus on differences in employer behavior across locations in the metropolitan area.

[32] Even within suburban areas, employers may choose to locate in areas that are far from black residential areas and not accessible by public transportation (Kain 1992).

politan areas we surveyed, we see from the data in table 4.8 that differences in both the demand and supply of minority labor between the central city and the suburbs vary from one metropolitan area to another. In particular, differences between central-city and suburban employers in the tendencies of firms to receive applications from blacks are relatively greater in Detroit and Boston than in Atlanta and Los Angeles. In fact, the applicant rates in the central city for blacks overall are roughly three times as high as in the suburbs in Detroit and Boston, while they are well under twice as high in Atlanta and Los Angeles. These differences parallel those noted in table 4.1 for employment, and this likely reflects the greater degree of residential segregation in Detroit and Boston (as well as the sprawling nature of the central city of Los Angeles and the heavy use of automobiles by blacks there).

Furthermore, differences in hiring ratios for blacks between central-city and suburban areas also appear more modest in Atlanta (and for black males in Boston) than in Detroit, perhaps indicating a greater degree of racial polarity and tensions in Detroit, or greater racial gaps in skill proficiency and credentials.[33]

Generally, there are distinct differences between black males and females in the industries and occupations to which they apply and in which they are hired, as revealed by the data in tables C.4 and C.5 of appendix C, in which results are pooled across metropolitan areas but presented separately for primary central-city and suburban areas.[34] Broadly speaking, black females are both more likely to apply and to be hired for jobs in the trade and service industries and for clerical, sales, and service jobs; black males are more likely to apply and be hired for jobs in manufacturing/construction and blue-collar jobs.

These parallels between the occupations and industries in which black males or females apply for work and those in which

[33] The greater similarity between suburban and central-city Atlanta in hiring rates for blacks may partly reflect the tendency for some firms in relatively suburban areas with central-city mailing addresses to be included as part of the primary central-city sample, as we noted in chapter 2.

[34] Since industry is a firm-wide measure but occupation is job-specific, we leave out firm-wide employment-to-applicant ratios in the latter table. Since the applicant rates are also firm-wide, these measures must be interpreted with some caution in the latter table. But firms reporting recent hiring in a particular occupation should also, on average, have more employment in those occupations overall than those firms that do not report such hiring.

Table 4.8 / Applicant and Hire Rates

	Atlanta			Boston			Detroit			Los Angeles		
	PCC[a]	SUB[b]	OTH[c]	PCC	SUB	OTH	PCC	SUB	OTH	PCC	SUB	OTH
Percent of Applicants Who Are												
Black Males	.276	.161	.232	.158	.058	.083	.299	.128	.316	.108	.132	.113
Black Females	.249	.136	.174	.128	.041	.089	.292	.110	.220	.074	.104	.148
Hispanics	.035	.024	.034	.085	.059	.159	.067	.022	.027	.425	.370	.302
Asians	.037	.022	.023	.047	.048	.057	.029	.035	.031	.121	.109	.088
Ratio of Employees to Applicants For												
Black Males	.670	.913	.823	.690	.660	.511	.702	.430	.487	.626	.428	.389
Black Females	.871	.772	.920	.805	.548	.685	1.010	.564	.623	1.042	.453	.297
Hispanics	.739	1.083	1.143	1.110	.967	.748	1.836	.955	.857	1.000	1.078	1.079
Asians	.650	.740	.487	.734	.873	.462	.276	.395	.332	1.471	.862	1.007
Ratio of Hires to Applicants For												
Black Males	.659	.665	.681	.462	.517	.253	.645	.430	.443	.444	.371	1.536
Black Females	.683	.794	1.000	.555	.244	.596	1.002	.782	.736	.716	.471	.223
Hispanics	1.000	1.250	.735	1.200	.814	2.108	.478	.938	1.279	1.042	.981	1.066
Asians	.595	.955	.565	.404	.854	.193	.069	.229	.935	1.548	.844	1.484

[a] Primary central city.
[b] Suburbs.
[c] Other areas, as defined in table 2.2.

they are hired imply that there is some *self-selection* among applicants—in other words, they are more likely to search for work where they think there are greater chances for success. This also implies that differences in employer demand across occupations and industries are *under*stated by observed differences in hiring ratios, relative to what they would be if applicants were more evenly distributed. Thus, efforts to increase the employment of blacks in jobs and in locations where they lag behind will take more than mere efforts to improve their "geographic access" to these jobs if many employers in these locations resist hiring the black applicants who manage to find them.

Furthermore, the tendency to hire black applicants in the suburbs seems relatively low in the retail trade and service sectors, and it is strikingly low there for black males in the clerical and sales occupations. This strongly suggests that employer discrimination in the suburbs may be related to the degree of employee contact with white customers, which is consistent with Becker's notion (1971) of customer-based discrimination.

MULTIVARIATE ANALYSIS OF EMPLOYMENT BY RACE AND GENDER

All of our tables thus far have presented data on the race and gender of new employees separately by individual characteristics and locations of firms and jobs. But it is likely that only some of these factors are the real determinants of the observed employment patterns, while others are merely correlated with these determinants and contribute very little on their own.

In order to sort out these possibilities, we estimated multivariate regression equations in which the *dependent variables* are the race and gender of the newly hired workers (for white and black males, and white and black females), and the *independent variables* are such characteristics as skill requirements, hiring requirements, and the like.

The functional form used for these equations is the binomial logistic (or logit) model, which is appropriate in cases where the dependent variable is categorical.[35] All samples were limited to non-

[35] Equations were estimated using maximum-likelihood procedures. While multinomial logits could have been used to simultaneously estimate the probabilities

college workers, and all equations estimated included controls for the metropolitan area and central city/suburban location of the firm, and for the age and education of the individual ultimately hired. Thus, we control more completely here for human capital differences across groups than we did in the simple comparisons presented earlier.

But other groups of independent variables have been added sequentially in four different specifications of each equation: (1) the daily task performance variables; (2) the various recruiting and screening measures, including self-reported employer attitudes and interview objectives; (3) other characteristics of jobs or firms, such as occupational and industrial categories, collective bargaining, establishment size, and the seasonal or temporary status of the job; and (4) the fractions of applicants and customers, respectively, who are black.

The reason for adding these variables sequentially is that many of them are quite highly correlated with each other, making a single specification unlikely to generate very meaningful results. Furthermore, there is as much risk of *over*controlling as there is of *under*controlling in each specification. For instance, the tasks needed on these jobs may well determine exactly which recruiting and hiring procedures are used, in which case controlling for the latter when estimating the effects of the former may be inappropriate. But to the extent that the former are not completely specified and that the latter may have independent effects on outcomes, the controls may be reasonable. Other questions about some of these variables (for example, their subjective nature and resulting biases from measurement error) also argue for alternative specifications in which they are sometimes included and sometimes not.

Likewise, controlling for such characteristics as occupation (and industry or establishment size) may be inappropriate if differences across these categories are embodied in the tasks and hiring procedures, while they may be appropriate if the latter have effects on outcomes that are independent of the former. This is especially true for the percentages of applicants and customers who are

---

for all four race-by-gender groups, separate binomial logits were instead estimated for each group due to their greater computational ease in cases where the number of independent variables is very large. Specifications for which the two were compared show very little substantive difference in results between the two.

Table 4.9 / Determinants of Hiring for Non-College Jobs by Demographic Group: Results of Significance Tests on Logit Estimates

	White Males				Black Males			
	1	2	3	4	1	2	3	4
1. Tasks (4)	104.40 .000	64.96 .000	17.40 .002	3.69 .450	52.97 .000	23.91 .000	14.77 .005	8.00 .091
2. Recruitment, screens, and employer attitudes (26)	—	89.91 .000	50.42 .003	35.52 .101	—	61.40 .000	34.50 .123	23.75 .534
3. Employer size (4)	—	—	10.40 .034	2.96 .565	—	—	13.62 .009	7.81 .099
4. Blacks as percent of applicants and customers (2)	—	—	—	14.45 .001	—	—	—	83.59 .000

	White Females				Black Females			
	1	2	3	4	1	2	3	4
1. Tasks (4)	240.29 .000	118.99 .000	30.44 .000	22.06 .000	45.16 .000	29.16 .000	13.63 .009	7.74 .102
2. Recruitment, screens, and attitudes (26)	—	135.53 .000	78.19 .000	62.48 .000	—	47.77 .006	30.40 .252	24.46 .493
3. Employer size (4)	—	—	8.31 .081	3.02 .555	—	—	14.32 .006	4.90 .298
4. Blacks as percent of applicants and customers (2)	—	—	—	47.09 .000	—	—	—	144.63 .000

NOTE: These results are based on binomial logit equations for the probability of hiring members of each demographic group. Each entry presents results from likelihood-ratio tests. The top one is the chi-squared value for the appropriate number of restrictions, and the bottom represents the significance level. All equations include MSA, central-city, age, and education dummies (as well as a constant), while the third and fourth equations also include occupation and industry dummies, a seasonal/temporary dummy, and the percent covered by collective bargaining.

black, which are particularly powerful as controls but very likely endogenous with respect to the observed employment outcomes as well as the other independent variables.[36]

Table 4.9 presents the results of likelihood-ratio tests for the

[36] For instance, the tendency of blacks to shop or apply for jobs at particular firms may partly depend on whether blacks are already employed there. The strong tendency noted above for blacks to self-select into jobs and firms where they have greater chances of getting hired also implies that this variable may overcontrol when estimating the effects of tasks, hiring screens, and the like. On the other hand, these controls allow for estimated effects on the other variables to be interpreted as lower bounds to the true effects of skill requirements, among other things, on employer demand.

significance of groups of independent variables in each equation, which include both chi-square values (for the appropriate number of variable restrictions) and significance levels for the variable groups.[37] (The estimated logit coefficients and standard errors themselves may be found in table C.6 in appendix C.)[38]

These results show that the task performance and hiring variables are each jointly significant at roughly the .10 level in most specifications. The task variables remain significant until we control for the presence of blacks among applicants and customers, and even then they remain significant at the .10–.20 level for all groups except white males. A similar pattern can be found among the hiring variables, though significance levels decline somewhat earlier and disappear totally with the last set of controls. Employer size also seems to have some independent effects on hiring outcomes, while black applicants and customers have very strong effects on these outcomes.

The coefficients in table C.6 in many ways confirm what we found in the summary data presented earlier and in the significance tests of the preceding table. In particular, the daily task performance variables are frequently significant individually, and are almost always negative for black males. In particular, daily use of arithmetic generally has strong negative effects on the hiring of blacks (and computer use hurts black males to some extent as well).

Among hiring criteria and procedures, experience and previous training requirements are most likely to limit the hiring of black males, while general experience requirements hurt black females the most. The importance of employers' skill requirements and the emphasis they place on particular credentials in limiting the employment prospects of minorities is confirmed here. On the other hand, recruiting methods, attitudes, and interviewing objectives show more mixed effects in these equations.

Of course, the presence of black applicants has strong effects

[37] The likelihood-ratio test in an equation estimated through maximum likelihood is comparable to an F-test for joint statistical significance of a group of independent variables in an equation estimated through ordinary least squares.

[38] To transform logit coefficients into partial effects on probabilities of outcomes, coefficients must be multiplied by $P * (1 - P)$, where P is the mean of the dependent variable. This implies that coefficients should generally be multiplied by roughly .2 and .1 for whites and blacks, respectively.

on the hiring of blacks (though these may be partly endogenous), and affirmative action effects look weaker after including other controls. Additionally, two other findings from table C.6 deserve mention: we find that black employment rates are significantly higher at *larger* establishments and at those that serve *black customers*, even after controlling for the racial composition of the hiring pool.

It is well known that large firms pay higher wages and benefits to employees than do smaller firms (see, for example, Brown, Hamilton, and Medoff 1990), and generate larger applicant pools (Holzer, Katz, and Krueger 1991). If anything, these characteristics should enable them to generate higher-quality applicant pools among both whites and minorities, which could just as easily lead them to hire fewer rather than more minorities.

Their tendency to hire more minorities, then, likely reflects other geographic or institutional differences between these firms and smaller ones. Perhaps it reflects their greater visibility in the community and a resulting fear of lawsuits and bad press; or perhaps it is their greater use of more formalized hiring procedures and personnel policies.[39]

Both larger firms and those with many black customers are more likely to be located in the primary central cities than in the suburbs, and these factors account at least partly for the greater tendencies of central-city firms to hire black applicants.[40] Furthermore, the effects of customer composition are highly consistent with the lower hiring of blacks (especially black males) in suburban sales and clerical jobs that we noted above, and with Becker's (1971) notion of customer-based discrimination. Thus, for both larger firms and those with many black customers, their greater tendencies to hire blacks likely reflect less employer discrimination relative to smaller firms and those with mostly white customers, which are concentrated in the suburbs.

Overall, the magnitudes of some of the effects described above

[39] See Holzer (1987b) for evidence that blacks are relatively more disadvantaged when using informal methods of jobseeking.

[40] The coefficient on primary central city in the equations reported in table C.6 is no longer significant once these variables are included, and it is reduced in magnitude by more than one-half.

do not look particularly small (though many vary a great deal across regression specifications). For instance, daily arithmetic use (when the coefficient is converted into a partial derivative, as described above) reduces employment of black males and females each by about 3–4.5 percentage points in the relevant jobs, which constitute about 30 percent of the sample. In at least some specifications, the effect of computers on the hiring of black males is even larger (5–6 percentage points in half of all jobs).

Whether such employment is actually eliminated or merely reallocated to other jobs (at lower wages) is not clear here, but relative to the overall probabilities of hiring blacks (roughly .10 for males and females each in this sample) these are not small effects. Given that these employer skill needs have probably risen over time, their estimated effects on employment are also consistent with the increasing relative earnings of women and decreasing earnings of blacks that we've observed over the past few decades (though we cannot measure the exact contributions of these changes over time in a single cross-section of firms).

Thus, even after controlling for racial differences in educational attainment, employer perceptions of racial and gender differences in abilities to perform tasks, in certain credentials, and in the preferences of their customers apparently lead them to hire blacks (and Hispanics) much less frequently in some jobs than others. The tendencies of blacks to apply for jobs more frequently in some firms (and geographic areas) than in others clearly have strong effects on these employment patterns as well.

CONCLUSIONS

When we look at employment patterns by race and gender across geographic areas, occupations, and industries, we see that blacks are relatively more likely to be employed in the central cities than in suburban areas; this distinction is more striking in some metropolitan areas (especially Detroit) than in others. We also find a growing tendency for Hispanics to capture traditional blue-collar and/or manufacturing work, while blacks are more concentrated in service jobs and industries.

The employment of blacks and Hispanics, especially males but also females, for certain jobs appears to be significantly limited by the tasks that must be performed daily (such as computer use and reading/writing), the credentials that these groups bring to the labor market, and particular attitudes and preferences of employers (such as their unwillingness to hire those with potential criminal backgrounds).

We find that blacks are more likely to apply to central-city employers, and that such employers are more likely than their suburban counterparts to hire black applicants. Given that task requirements are generally a bit higher in the central city than in the suburban areas, while the relative credentials of black applicants in the central city are probably not higher, the data strongly suggest greater discriminatory behavior by suburban employers.

Moreover, it appears likely that employers prefer black female to black male applicants, and Hispanic applicants to black applicants—even though Hispanics appear to have greater deficiencies in at least some skills and credentials. These employer preferences may well explain the growing preponderance of Hispanics in manufacturing and blue-collar jobs, in which cognitive/interactive skill and educational requirements are not as high as in other sectors. Hispanic applicants also seemed less hampered than black applicants by the growing concentration of such jobs in the suburbs.

When we use multivariate regression analysis to analyze these different factors simultaneously at the firm level, controlling for differences in age and the educational attainment of workers, the importance of task performance and particular credentials in most cases is confirmed, as are the influences of such other factors as employer size and the racial composition of both customers and job applicants. The employer-size and customer effects are consistent with the greater preference among central-city employers for black applicants, and appear likely to reflect greater discriminatory practices among smaller and/or suburban employers.

Overall, then, we find that employer skill requirements appear to have important effects on the employment prospects of blacks and Hispanics, and of less-educated and less-skilled workers more generally. These effects have probably grown in magnitude in recent years. Problems of geographic location and discrimination also appear to impede the employment prospects of blacks.

Workers who are particularly lacking in labor market skills and credentials, especially black workers, and those whose access to suburban labor markets is most limited, are the most likely to have difficulties gaining employment in the short term. This is likely to be true not only for males but also for females who have poor skills and credentials—such as long-term AFDC recipients. Even if members of these groups are able to find employment, their earnings are likely to be particularly limited.

5 / What Wages Are Less-Educated Workers Paid?

The earnings of workers without college degrees declined significantly in the United States over the past two decades. At the same time, the gaps in earnings between those with and without college degrees, between whites and minorities, and between age groups widened. Earnings inequality *within* each of these groups rose as well. The earnings gap between men and women narrowed, though it remains substantial.[1]

According to much of the literature on these issues, these developments reflect a growing demand for skills in the workforce. However, this literature rarely documents the *exact* workplace skills that are needed (especially by those without college degrees) and even less frequently links these skills to the wages paid to different groups of workers.[2] Furthermore, very little of this litera-

[1]See the literature cited in the notes 1 and 2 in chapter 1 for more evidence on these issues.

[2]An exception is Krueger (1993), who has demonstrated a link between rising use of computers and wage differentials between workers. Other studies (for example, Blackburn and Neumark 1993; Murnane, Willett, and Levy 1995) have analyzed the link between rising earnings gaps and general cognitive skills as measured by the Armed Forces Qualifying Test (AFQT), though the issue of how these cognitive skills are used in the workplace is not dealt with in these studies. In contrast, some of the studies referred to earlier that document workplace skill needs more carefully (for example, the SCANS report of the U.S. Department of Labor) rarely link these to wages. Finally, the studies by Juhn *et al.* (1993), and Card and Lemieux (1994) provide

ture is based on data from *firms*, with which the effects of employer personnel policies and occupational characteristics on earnings can be directly evaluated.[3]

In this chapter we first consider the *starting* wages earned by high school graduates and dropouts among the different race and gender groups who were hired by the firms in our study.[4] We then analyze the determinants of these wages, focusing specifically on the factors considered in the previous two chapters: task performance on the job, employer hiring practices, and other characteristics of jobs and firms. The extent to which these factors affect wages, and can account for observed differences across race and gender groups, is the primary focus of this work. Again, the work presented here is based on a single cross-section of data, but some limited inferences about causes of changes over time can be made as well.

WAGES OF WORKERS WITH HIGH SCHOOL EDUCATION OR LESS

The data presented in table 5.1 on starting hourly and weekly wages for the various race-by-gender groups are shown for the primary central cities and suburbs of each of the four metropolitan areas we surveyed (though small sample sizes precluded showing results for Hispanics and Asians in many places). All data are sample-weighted as described in chapter 2.

The results reveal several major findings. As we have seen,

---

little observable evidence of skills, inferring them primarily from observed movements in wages for different groups.

[3]Exceptions include Groshen (1991) and Davis and Haltiwanger (1990), both of which measure earnings differences between and within firms and how they have grown over time. A few earlier papers of mine (Holzer 1990a, 1990b) looked at wage differences across firms using the EOPP employer data from the early 1980s, though few job-specific measures of skills were available there.

[4]Some data are also available on the *current* wages of workers—that is, wages earned by workers at the time of the survey. However, the measures were very highly correlated with the starting wages of these workers, particularly since very little time had elapsed since the time of hiring in most cases. Smaller sample sizes, at least partly caused by turnover, also made the current wages less useful here. But given our focus on starting wages for a sample of low tenure employees, we necessarily abstract from important issues such as wage growth and turnover as determinants of earnings differences across groups. Some results may also differ from those described in other studies, which are based on broader samples of workers with different levels of tenure.

Table 5.1 / Starting Wages by Race/Gender and Location for High School Graduates or Less

	Atlanta		Boston		Detroit		Los Angeles	
	PCC	SUB	PCC	SUB	PCC	SUB	PCC	SUB
Hourly Wages (in dollars)								
Males								
Whites	7.88	7.98	11.02	9.80	8.91	7.81	10.20	9.37
	(2.03)	(2.53)	(3.28)	(3.45)	(3.80)	(3.64)	(2.40)	(4.30)
Blacks	7.66	6.66	11.88	8.20	7.37	7.65	8.78	8.01
	(2.09)	(1.89)	(4.13)	(2.98)	(2.07)	(3.16)	(1.47)	(3.33)
Hispanics	—	—	—	7.35	—	—	7.16	7.78
				(1.35)			(2.96)	(3.13)
Asians	—	—	—	7.73	—	—	7.51	7.79
				(2.82)			(3.84)	(2.01)
Females								
Whites	8.35	7.64	9.44	8.14	7.25	6.75	11.70	9.71
	(2.89)	(2.56)	(2.65)	(2.89)	(4.84)	(2.47)	(2.77)	(4.00)
Blacks	7.83	5.83	7.42	6.73	5.70	5.53	8.69	7.30
	(2.61)	(1.16)	(2.49)	(1.22)	(1.57)	(1.59)	(2.03)	(2.28)
Hispanics	—	—	—	6.95	—	—	7.30	7.66
				(2.30)			(3.01)	(3.56)
Asians	—	—	—	6.40	—	—	—	5.96
				(4.30)				(3.36)

Weekly Wages (in dollars)								
Males								
Whites	370.99	313.84	443.21	389.14	413.31	316.52	407.80	376.34
	(94.42)	(125.53)	(142.34)	(185.37)	(181.47)	(202.53)	(95.88)	(189.36)
Blacks	312.29	276.50	465.65	175.18	294.91	353.84	332.41	289.73
	(97.75)	(113.29)	(181.18)	(96.07)	(113.82)	(208.03)	(34.33)	(14.62)
Hispanics	—	—	—	270.10	—	—	289.80	311.48
				(56.34)			(118.51)	(146.85)
Asians	—	—	—	297.85	—	—	227.63	301.52
				(126.26)			(44.80)	(128.41)
Females								
Whites	326.51	273.74	362.93	295.98	262.84	226.52	467.98	356.97
	(126.96)	(122.72)	(108.38)	(134.91)	(141.88)	(122.94)	(110.87)	(182.46)
Blacks	294.34	197.06	284.30	323.94	200.65	186.85	314.29	245.83
	(119.20)	(69.11)	(113.97)	(147.09)	(80.85)	(92.37)	(99.60)	(123.20)
Hispanics	—	—	—	230.57	—	—	282.82	284.55
				(98.36)			(130.71)	(159.05)
Asians	—	—	—	235.52	—	—	—	192.70
				(196.98)				(88.35)

wage levels in Boston and Los Angeles are higher than those in Detroit and especially higher than those in Atlanta. It is, of course, widely known that average wage levels differ across regions and metropolitan areas at any point in time, reflecting local economic conditions, housing costs, industrial concentrations, nonwage amenities, and the like.[5] For our purposes, the important thing is that the relative concentration of blacks in Atlanta and Detroit will lower their wages overall, while the concentration of Hispanics and Asians in Boston and especially in Los Angeles will raise theirs. Controls for these intermetropolitan wage differences must therefore be included in any analysis of wage differences across racial groups.

Another finding from table 5.1 confirms what we observed in chapter 2: most groups of workers are paid more when they work in the primary central city than when they work in the suburbs. But there are also some clear exceptions to this rule: Hispanics and Asians in Los Angeles generally earn more in the suburbs, as do black males in Detroit.[6]

The higher wages of whites working in the central city (even when controlling for differences in personal skills and industrial distributions) have often been attributed to compensation for commute times for those who live in the suburbs (see Madden 1985; Zax 1991). If the central city is viewed as a particularly unattractive location (perhaps because of crime, racial tensions, or other factors), additional compensation may be required; indeed, the percentage central-city premium for white males is highest in Detroit.

On the other hand, for minorities whose residences are more heavily concentrated in the central-city areas, there is less need for commute-time compensation. In fact, the spatial (geographic) factors discussed above that prevent many black central-city residents from gaining suburban employment may also lower their wages when they work in the central city, as a relatively large supply of less-skilled labor is "crowded" into a limited number of

[5]Differences across local areas in wages are discussed, among other places, in Blanchard and Katz (1992), Blanchflower and Oswald (1990), and Rosen (1986). The literature frequently distinguishes between "equilibrium" and "disequilibrium" differences, where the latter are temporary responses to demand shifts that are mitigated by equilibrating factors such as migration across areas.

[6]In a few additional cases, the hourly wage is higher for a particular group in one area, while the weekly wage is higher in the other.

jobs.[7] These factors might well account for the lower wages of black males in central-city Detroit relative to those in suburban areas.[8]

When we compare the earnings of racial and gender groups within areas, we generally find that white males are the most highly paid group and minority females are the lowest paid. Within locations, black males generally earn more on an hourly basis than Hispanic males do, though the differences are generally not large in percentage terms; on a weekly basis, the gap in earnings between black and Hispanic males is even smaller, indicating fewer hours worked by blacks.[9] Wage differences between black males and white females are more varied.

These results are generally consistent with most analyses of earnings differentials by race and gender. However, our survey results show that these differences appear even when we focus only on employees with no education beyond high school and no job tenure; therefore, the earnings differences illustrated in table 5.1 clearly cannot be attributed to these "human capital" factors.[10]

Another finding is that most racial and gender earnings gaps are larger when measured by weekly than by hourly wages. Differences across groups in the average number of hours worked per week thus magnify differences in hourly earnings to generate even larger differences at the weekly level. For females, the differences in hours per week may be *supply*-based, since women may choose to work fewer hours than men in order to care for their

[7]See, for example, Ihlanfeldt (1994) for evidence on wage gradients favoring less-educated blacks in the suburbs. Recent evidence on the issue of "crowding" for blacks appears in Hirsch and MacPherson (1994).

[8]We would expect that the relatively highly skilled black workers who live in the central city are the ones most likely to commute to work in the suburbs. This might be even more true in Detroit than in other metropolitan areas, since highly skilled black workers may be more likely to live in the suburbs as well in the latter.

[9]These wage differences also do not adjust for the higher educational levels of blacks. Wage gaps between black and Hispanic females show no consistent pattern at all.

[10]Since the sample is conditioned on employment, the dropout rates among the whites and blacks in this sample differ only marginally; educational attainments beyond high school differ more significantly but are not represented in the sample used here, which excludes workers in jobs that require college. Quality differences in education and general work experience prior to being hired may differ more substantially for the blacks and whites included here.

Table 5.2 / Wages by Race/Gender for Manufacturing/Non-Manufacturing Jobs Among High School Graduates or Less

	White Male		Black Male		Hispanic Male	
	Mfg	Other	Mfg	Other	Mfg	Other
Hourly Wages	9.82	8.20	7.61	7.42	7.87	7.17
	(4.08)	(3.17)	(2.37)	(2.56)	(3.04)	(2.73)
Weekly Wages	415.61	316.45	319.20	297.05	324.75	274.91
	(181.47)	(158.62)	(99.11)	(133.23)	(142.35)	(124.90)

children; this is somewhat less likely to be true for racial differences in hours among males.[11]

In table 5.2 we present wages for race and gender groups with a high school education or less, broken down by workers in manufacturing industries and all other workers. Given the apparent disappearance of such jobs for black males and their relative growth among Hispanics, it is important to find out whether the latter benefit from the wage premiums that have traditionally been associated with such work.

The results show that starting wage premiums in manufacturing are more substantial for white males than for any other group. This premium is worth roughly 20 percent in terms of their wages on an hourly basis, and over 30 percent in terms of their wages on a weekly basis. In contrast, the hourly premium is 10 percent or less for all other groups and roughly 20 percent or less for weekly wages. Among these other groups, white females and Hispanic males earn the most substantial premiums in manufacturing; for black males the premium is quite low (roughly 3 percent and 7 percent for hourly and weekly wages, respectively); and for minority females, the wages in manufacturing appear to be slightly *lower* than in other industries at the hourly level and fairly comparable at the weekly level.

To some extent, these findings reflect differences in where each group now works among specific industries and occupations

[11] The difference between supply- and demand-based hours of work parallels that between "voluntary" and "involuntary" part-time work, where both have grown over time for women (Blank 1990).

	White Female		Black Female		Hispanic Female	
	Mfg	Other	Mfg	Other	Mfg	Other
Hourly Wages	8.72	7.91	6.00	6.79	6.86	7.52
	(3.03)	(3.05)	(1.50)	(2.23)	(1.57)	(3.34)
Weekly Wages	339.50	280.48	229.74	234.95	273.02	268.64
	(136.57)	(139.44)	(74.85)	(110.80)	(68.92)	(152.08)

within the manufacturing sector; thus, black females are somewhat more likely than others to work in *non*durable manufacturing industries, where wage premiums have traditionally been lower, and white females are much more likely than black or Hispanic females to have clerical occupations within this sector.[12] The occupations and industries in which each group works in manufacturing might also have changed over time, though some changes in earnings have no doubt occurred *within* many of the occupations and industries as well.

Whatever the cause, these findings generally indicate that manufacturing employment no longer holds out the promise of higher earnings to minorities, especially blacks, that it traditionally has. For black males, the dwindling employment in this sector, and the disappearance of the substantial earnings premium attached to it, implies that a once-promising avenue for advancement for those without higher education or particularly strong cognitive/interactive skills no longer exists. For Hispanic males, a significant wage premium still exists in manufacturing, but the wage level is hardly better than that obtained by black males in this sector.

Finally, the curious ability shown by white males to continue to command the highest starting wages in manufacturing—even when we hold constant for education (as well as job tenure)—

[12] The fractions of black females employed in non-college jobs who work in durable and non-durable manufacturing are .04 and .08, respectively; for all other race-by-gender groups the fractions in each are much closer to each other in magnitude (with some, such as white and Hispanic males, having slightly higher fractions in durables). The fraction of white females in manufacturing with clerical jobs is about .54, where comparable fractions for black and Hispanic females are .24 and .14, respectively.

implies that they continue to have greater access to the best jobs there, likely reflecting some combination of superior unobserved skills, contacts, and/or discrimination in the hiring process.

MULTIVARIATE ANALYSIS OF WAGE DETERMINATION

We now turn to a multivariate regression analysis of these wage differences across groups and across jobs and firms more generally.

We have estimated regression equations in which the dependent variable is the log of the weekly starting wage of the last person hired in each firm. The independent variables included are the same as those used in the previous chapter when estimating employment determinants (for example, MSA and central-city/suburban locations within it, as well as the age and education of the worker hired), though they also include dummies for race-by-gender group as well. Thus, the results presented in the first few tables are from regressions that pool workers from the various groups, while results from separate equations by race and gender are presented later. The samples include all workers in jobs that do not require college degrees. All equations here are estimated by ordinary least squares.

Table 5.3 presents results of significance tests (F-Tests) for groups of variables, while table 5.4 presents the actual coefficients (and standard errors) on the variables of interest.[13] As in chapter 4, we use four specifications; in fact, tables 5.3 and 5.4 correspond directly to tables 4.9 and C.6 (in appendix C), except that significance tests for the recruitment and hiring procedures are now presented for more detailed groups of variables as well as for one large aggregate.[14]

The results in table 5.3 show that virtually each group of variables has a significant effect on wages in each specification, with the exception of the testing variables. Thus, wages vary significantly according to the tasks performed on the job, the hiring procedures used, employer size, and the percentages of employ-

[13] F-tests are used instead of chi-squared tests, since the estimation technique used here is OLS instead of maximum likelihood.

[14] Another difference is that the fractions of blacks are now presented out of employees rather than applicants, with black males and females pooled into one group.

Table 5.3 / Significance Tests for Log (Weekly Wage) Equations, Non-College Jobs—Pooled Sample

	1	2	3	4
1. Tasks (4)	54.23	27.60	16.86	12.87
	.000	.000	.000	.000
2. Recruitment, screening, and employer attitudes:		18.75	11.50	8.89
Total (26)	—	.000	.000	.000
Individual Groups		13.20	9.12	5.57
Recruitment (9)	—	.000	.000	.000
Requirements (5)		35.91	23.30	17.44
	—	.000	.000	.000
Interview (5)		10.17	2.43	2.79
	—	.000	.033	.016
Tests (2)		5.96	1.04	1.14
	—	.003	.353	.319
Attitudes (3)		10.34	12.86	12.12
	—	.000	.000	.000
3. Employer size (4)			8.26	2.63
	—	—	.000	.033
4. Blacks as percent of employees and customers (2)				2.71
	—	—	—	.067

NOTE. These results are based on equations that all contain dummies for MSA, central city, race and gender, age group (16–24, 25–34), and educational attainment of employee hired. The top entry represents the F-value for the appropriate number of restrictions, while the bottom represents significance level.

ees as well as customers who are black. These results hold even after controlling for the worker's age and education, as well as occupation and industry (in the final two specifications).

The results in table 5.4 show more specifically the effects of these variables on weekly wage levels. For instance, daily reading/writing and computer use have quite significant effects on wages—the former ranging from 13 to 23 percent, the latter from 8 to 17 percent.[15] In contrast, dealing with customers has a negative effect, at least until we control for occupation. Significant differentials are also associated with certain recruitment methods, though these may be endogenous to some degree.[16]

[15] The latter magnitudes are quite consistent with what Krueger (1993) obtains in his study of computer use and wages.

[16] In other words, the recruiting method may be chosen to generate workers of a given skill level who merit the pay provided, rather than the reverse.

Table 5.4 / Determinants of Weekly Wages for Non-College Jobs: Coefficient (Standard Errors) of Pooled Equations

	1	2	3	4
Task				
Customers	−.165**	−.084**	.004	.028
	(.023)	(.024)	(.025)	(.032)
Read/Write	.226**	.168**	.125**	.149**
	(.021)	(.020)	(.020)	(.025)
Arithmetic	.013	.012	.016	.010
	(.022)	(.020)	(.020)	(.025)
Computers	.167**	.107**	.091**	.076**
	(.023)	(.021)	(.022)	(.028)
Recruiting Method				
Help-Wanted		−.192**	−.104**	−.056
	—	(.050)	(.049)	(.059)
Newspaper Ad		.028	.017	.056*
	—	(.029)	(.028)	(.034)
Walk-in		−.224**	−.184**	−.159**
	—	(.033)	(.033)	(.042)
Current Employee		−.069**	−.072**	−.053*
	—	(.029)	(.028)	(.036)
State Employee Service		−.026	−.100**	−.033
	—	(.057)	(.056)	(.076)
Private Employment Service		.098**	.065*	.107*
	—	(.048)	(.047)	(.068)
Community Agency		−.014	−.014	.067
	—	(.081)	(.077)	(.121)
School		−.159**	−.182**	−.178**
	—	(.051)	(.050)	(.062)
Union		.462**	.352**	.371**
	—	(.107)	(.103)	(.153)
Affirmative Action		.034**	−.003	−.018
	—	(.020)	(.019)	(.025)
Require				
High School Diploma		.123*	.077**	.085**
	—	(.024)	(.024)	(.030)
General Experience		.056**	.040**	.034
	—	(.023)	(.022)	(.028)
Specific Experience		.151**	.125**	.132**
	—	(.023)	(.022)	(.028)
References		−.011	.011	.006
	—	(.022)	(.021)	(.027)
Vocational Education or Training		.096**	.083**	.104**
	—	(.021)	(.021)	(.026)
Would Hire				
GED/Government Training		.020	.012	−.011
	—	(.028)	(.027)	(.041)
Criminal		.072**	.077**	.080**
	—	(.020)	(.020)	(.026)

Table 5.4 / *(Continued)*

	1	2	3	4
Short-Term, Part-Time		−.098**	−.104**	−.134**
	—	(.021)	(.020)	(.025)
Interview—Yes		−.007	−.009	−.018
	—	(.030)	(.029)	(.037)
Interview—Looks for				
Appearance/Neatness		−.104**	−.055**	−.049**
	—	(.021)	(.021)	(.026)
Verbal/English		−.027	−.017	−.062**
	—	(.024)	(.024)	(.030)
Politeness		−.069**	−.019	−.031
	—	(0.26)	(.026)	(.033)
Motivation		.024	.023	.044*
	—	(.021)	(.021)	(.027)
Test				
Physical		.065**	.009	.022
	—	(.028)	(.028)	(.037)
Work Sample/Other		.027	.024	.027
	—	(.022)	(.021)	(.027)
Check Education/Criminal Record		.018	−.004	−.013
	—	(.020)	(.019)	(.025)
Occupation	—	—	yes	yes
Industry	—	—	yes	yes
Seasonal/Temporary			−.174**	−.199**
	—	—	(.032)	(.041)
Collective Bargaining			.117**	.110**
	—	—	(.031)	(.039)
Size				
1–20			−.170**	−.131**
	—	—	(.034)	(.048)
21–50			−.095**	−.090**
	—	—	(.036)	(.050)
51–100			−.161**	−.114**
	—	—	(.038)	(.052)
101–500			−.031	−.019
	—	—	(.033)	(.047)
% of Employees Who Are Black				−.012
	—	—	—	(.044)
% of Customers Who Are Black				−.141**
	—	—	—	(.066)
N	2381	2323	2110	1406
R^2	.258	.392	.497	.512
$\bar{R}^2$	.252	.379	.480	.487

NOTE: One asterisk (*) indicates significance at only the .20 level in a two-tailed test, while two asterisks (**) indicate at least .10 significance.

Among the requirements for being hired, we find that significant wage differentials are paid in jobs that require high school degrees, general experience, specific experience, and prior vocational education or training. The returns to specific experience (13–15 percent) and prior training (8–10 percent) are largest in magnitude, even after controlling for occupation and industry.

Employers that would accept workers with only short-term and/or part-time experience pay 10–13 percent less, and those in which appearance and neatness are critical pay 5–10 percent less. Surprisingly, employers who would accept those with criminal records pay 7–8 percent *more*. Less surprising, seasonal or temporary jobs and those under collective-bargaining agreements pay less and more, respectively, while large establishments also pay more. Finally, even when we control for location within the central city and MSA as well as for all other observable job and employer characteristics, our analysis shows that firms with larger fractions of black customers pay significantly less to their employees. Why this is so is not clear. It may, for example, reflect lower prices charged by firms that cater to a relatively lower-income clientele. Whatever the explanation, it adds to the hurdles black workers face in obtaining earnings of the level paid to comparable white workers.

To what extent do these observable characteristics of jobs and employers account for the differences in wages paid to workers by race and gender? One way to answer this would be to compare the magnitudes of coefficients on race-by-gender dummy variables across these specifications, to see the extent to which the variables added in each case can account for observed group differences. But this approach would rely on estimates from pooled samples across the different groups. In fact, F-tests performed on pooled versus separate estimated equations for these groups clearly reject the pooling strategy in all specifications, implying that the effects of the various determinants on earnings differ significantly across groups.

We therefore present some additional results from equations that have been estimated separately for black and white males and females. In table 5.5 we present estimates of the extent to which the differences in weekly wages between white males and the other three groups in non-college jobs can be accounted for by differences in the observed attributes between them.

Table 5.5 / Separate Log (Weekly Wage) Equations for Non-College Jobs by Race/Gender: Predicted Differences (Relative to White Males)

		Attributable to X's		Attributable to β's	
	Overall Difference	1	2	1	2
Black Males	.173	—	—	—	—
Specification No. 2	—	.097	.051	.130	.087
Specification No. 4	—	.102	.173	−.011	.060
White Females	.181	—	—	—	—
Specification No. 2	—	.057	−.080	.253	.119
Specification No. 4	—	.075	−.038	.192	.079
Black Females	.350	—	—	—	—
Specification No. 2	—	.127	.025	.325	.223
Specification No. 4	—	.212	.128	.203	.119

NOTE: Column 1 represents calculations using coefficients (β) or attributes (X) of white males as the base, while column 2 uses those of the relevant race/gender group. Estimates are based on sample-weighted means.

The method used to measure these differences is the well-known decomposition of group earnings differences developed by Blinder (1973) and Oaxaca (1973), in which the values of attributes (or independent variables) of one group are weighted by wage returns to these attributes (or coefficients) of another group, and then the predicted wage values are compared to actual mean wages of each group.

If, for instance, the attributes of minorities/females (and their jobs) weighted by estimated coefficients for white males generate predicted wages that are fairly close to the actual wages of the former, we infer that these attributes account for much of the observed wage differences between groups; while if the predicted values are closer to the actual wages of the latter, we infer that differences in coefficients (which reflect differences in market treatment of observable attributes, perhaps because of discrimination) account for most of the group differences.

In table 5.5 we present such calculations based on equations estimated separately across the four groups, using two of the specifications described above: the second (including tasks as well as recruiting and hiring behaviors and attitudes) and the fourth (including occupations, industries, establishment size, the existence of collective bargaining agreements, and the racial composition of the firm's customers and employees).

We present the percentage wage differences between white males and each other group that are accounted for by the differences in the attributes and in the coefficients across groups, where each is compared to the overall mean difference between the groups. Since we obtain different estimates based on exactly which group's coefficients we use with which group's attributes, we present each calculation two ways: once using attributes or coefficients of white males as the base, and once using those of the other groups as the base.

According to the equations in table 5.5, the results of this exercise vary substantially according to which specification of the wage equation is used and which group's attributes/coefficients are used as the base. But generally the results show that differences in observable attributes of workers and jobs account for quite significant fractions of the wage differences between white and black males; this is somewhat less true for differences between white males and black females; while it is least of all true for those between white males and females.

In fact, half or more of the difference between white and black males is accounted for in three of the four calculations, with one of them (the one that uses the most independent variables and the coefficients of black males) accounting for the entire difference. In contrast, no more than about 40 percent of the difference between white males and females is ever accounted for, and in the two calculations that use coefficients of the females, the fractions of the differences accounted for are actually *negative* (that is, the calculations actually predict higher wages for the females).

These results are not too surprising when one considers the results discussed in chapter 4: that white females were most likely to be hired into jobs that require the tasks and use the hiring procedures considered here, while black (and Hispanic) males were the least likely. Given that there appear to be positive effects of most of these job characteristics on wages, it is little wonder that these equations predict that white women should be highly paid and that black males should not be.

The simplest reading of the results, then, is that the relatively low wages of black males are explained primarily by their attributes; that those of white women are explained primarily by discrimination; and that the very low wages of black women are explained by some combination of the two.

Of course, this reading may well be too simple; perhaps it is discriminatory hiring that keeps black males out of jobs that require skills, and perhaps there are other characteristics of workers and their jobs, unobserved in these data, that really explain why men are paid more than women. These unobserved characteristics may to some extent involve the *choices* women make regarding the characteristics of jobs they want, rather than only the barriers they face on the demand side of the market.[17]

Nevertheless, these results imply that differences between the (perceived) characteristics of workers and the requirements of jobs that we have observed can account for much of the observed *wage* differences between whites and blacks, whereas discrimination is a more plausible explanation of the starting wage differences that remain between males and females.[18] These results stand in sharp contrast to those noted in the earlier chapter on *employment* (or hiring), where discrimination against blacks (especially in smaller and/or suburban firms with mostly white customers) seemed fairly pronounced.[19] Employers thus seem more reluctant to hire black males at any wage, while for white females there is obviously no such concern.[20]

[17] The issue of whether low wages or occupational segregation among women results from their own choices or from demand-side barriers is a fundamental one in the literature, especially when policy options such as "comparable worth" are debated. For instance, women may choose jobs that require little on-the-job training if they plan to exit the labor force to have or raise children; they might also choose traditionally female jobs if they are more comfortable in these or prefer their non-wage attributes, despite the lower wages they provide. For more evidence and discussion on these issues, see Gunderson (1989), Killingsworth (1990), and Sorensen (1994).

[18] These results confirm those found by O'Neill (1990), Ferguson (1993), and Neal and Johnson (1994), in which scores on the AFQT test accounted for much of the *wage* difference between whites and blacks.

[19] Neal and Johnson (1994) also find that their measures of cognitive ability explain substantially fewer of the racial gaps in employment than in wages.

[20] These results are at least consistent with (though they do not prove) the argument of Bloch (1994) and others, who have suggested that EEO activities on behalf of blacks may simply have replaced wage discrimination with employment discrimination against them. If more substantial hurdles are being applied to blacks at the hiring stage, we would also expect to find those who actually become employed to be relatively higher in quality (and thus earning higher relative wages) than we otherwise would find.

We note that the labor market rewards to the skill requirements of jobs, their relatively greater prevalence among jobs held by females, and the presumed growth over time in the labor market demand for these skills are consistent with the narrowing of the male-female wage difference and the widening of the black-white wage difference that has been observed over the previous two decades (Blau and Kahn 1994; Bound and Holzer 1995). Thus, although the market rewards to these skills and employer behaviors have not fully closed the male-female wage gap, they have apparently reduced that gap significantly.

We also note that, when we performed these calculations for Hispanic males and females, comparable results emerged—the lower wages of males are more completely accounted for by task requirements, hiring behavior, and other characteristics of firms and jobs than are those of females. Indeed, given the strong reluctance of employers to hire Hispanic males for jobs requiring formal education and the performance of certain tasks, their relatively low wages are of little surprise.

There are also some interesting findings in the underlying wage equations that generated these results and in how they differ across the groups considered here. In table 5.6 we present results from significance tests on groups of variables comparable to those presented in table 5.3 for the pooled samples but presented separately here for the four race-by-sex groups. To limit the amount of data shown, we show only the two specifications used in the previous table. The actual coefficients and standard errors from these estimated equations appear in table D.1 of appendix D.

The results in table 5.6 show that tasks and employer hiring requirements and behavior have significant effects on the wages earned by most racial and gender groups. As was the case earlier, these effects are weaker in the fourth specification than in the second, especially for white females. Employer size matters significantly only for the earnings of black males, and the percentage of blacks among employees and customers matters for those of black males and females.

Table D.1 also reveals some interesting differences across groups in returns to job and employer attributes. While all groups draw some reward for daily reading/writing on the job, only white males get significant returns for the use of arithmetic, and only white females get significant returns for computer use.

Table 5.6 / Separate Log (Wage) Equations: Significance Tests

	White Males		Black Males		White Females		Black Females	
	2	4	2	4	2	4	2	4
1. Tasks (4)	6.65	2.50	13.29	4.00	2.51	1.47	4.70	1.88
	.000	.043	.000	.003	.043	.219	.001	.118
2. Recruitment, screening, and employer	6.20	2.98	5.21	3.10	2.73	1.02	3.25	1.61
attitudes (26)	.000	.000	.000	.000	.000	.449	.000	.050
Recruitment	3.14	1.28	3.93	1.47	1.24	.75	4.13	1.52
	.001	.248	.000	.156	.272	.651	.000	.158
Requirements	16.09	6.26	8.02	3.64	2.58	.89	1.99	1.22
	.000	.000	.000	.003	.027	.491	.081	.303
Attitudes	2.48	2.76	4.81	8.39	1.28	.69	2.41	1.85
	.060	.043	.003	.000	.281	.563	.068	.143
Interviews	4.18	2.71	2.38	.64	3.58	1.43	2.56	1.20
	.001	.021	.037	.666	.004	.224	.028	.315
Tests	2.31	.39	1.43	.38	2.40	.18	3.37	.33
	.100	.677	.240	.672	.093	.835	.036	.719
3. Employer size (4)		.75		2.76		.14		.77
	—	.557	—	.027	—	.969	—	.547
4. Blacks as percentage of employees		.09		4.91		.42		2.90
and customers (2)	—	.910	—	.010	—	.656	—	.059

NOTE: See table 5.3.

We also note that white males get the highest rewards for specific experience and for prior vocational education and training, where they also do relatively well at the hiring stage (as we saw in chapter 4). These two observable dimensions of skills or credentials therefore appear to account for at least some of the relatively high wages earned by white males in these jobs, though their relatively high rewards to these attributes remain a bit of a puzzle. Both white and black males also obtain larger rewards from collective bargaining than females of either race.

Finally, we note that both the percentages of employees and customers who are black have large negative effects on the earnings of black males, while the latter has a smaller negative effect for black females. Why these should affect males more than females also remains a puzzle.

CONCLUSIONS

When we analyze the starting wages of different race-by-gender groups in the non-college jobs in which they have been hired, we find, as expected, that white males have the highest wages of these groups, while black and Hispanic females have the lowest. Black males earn more than do Hispanic males, though not more than white females in most cases.

White males also continue to earn the most substantial wage premiums from employment in manufacturing, while for most minority groups (except Hispanic males) these premiums are low or even negative. Given the low employment rates and the low wage returns for blacks in this sector, manufacturing is no longer an area in which substantial numbers of less-educated males can hope to earn relatively high wages.

When we use multivariate regressions to analyze the effects of tasks, hiring procedures, and the like on wages on a sample pooling workers from all groups, we find that the various tasks and hiring requirements (such as having a high school diploma, specific experience, or prior training) all have significant effects on weekly wages.

When we estimate separate equations across groups and use these to try to account for differences in observed wages, we find that the job and employer attributes that we observe do a fairly good job of accounting for the relatively low wages of black males, but they do much less well in accounting for the low wages of white females relative to white males (and somewhat less well in accounting for those of black females).

In other words, the gaps between the skills employers want and those they perceive among blacks are important determinants of the lower *wages* of the latter, while the relatively low wages earned by white females are more puzzling and are perhaps more attributable to discrimination. This stands in sharp contrast to the picture that emerges regarding differences in *employment,* where our results suggest continued discrimination against blacks (especially males) but not against females in general. On the other hand, it seems likely that the shift in labor demand toward these skills over time has benefited females relative to males and has helped to reduce the gap in earnings between them in recent years.

Finally, we find some differences across groups in the extent to which these job/employer characteristics translate into higher wages. Thus, white females are most heavily rewarded for the use of computers, and white males earn the largest returns for specific experience and prior training. Black males are penalized the most by working in establishments that hire many black workers or serve many black customers.

Overall, employer skill requirements and their behavior in meeting these requirements have some important effects on the earnings of minorities. Improving the skills and credentials of blacks and Hispanics in the workforce would no doubt improve their ability to land jobs that pay higher wages, though the problem of discriminatory employer perceptions remains a concern.

On the other hand, while the apparent shift in market demand toward the skills analyzed here has benefited females to date, further skill enhancement of this type holds out little hope to non-college women (especially among whites) who are already well-prepared in this regard when they enter the labor market. To improve their earnings prospects even further, other approaches (such as further limiting discrimination or providing more support for child care) may be necessary.

6 / Summary of Findings and Policy Implications

There is no doubt that enormous changes have occurred on the demand side of the labor market in recent years. These changes have apparently reduced the earnings and employment opportunities available to minorities and less-educated workers. But, despite all of the discussion and indirect evidence presented on such changes to date, we have lacked direct evidence at the micro level on employers and their demand for less-skilled labor.

In this volume we have presented such evidence on the characteristics of employers and jobs that are available to workers who do not have college degrees. The data are from a recently completed telephone survey of over 3,000 employers in four major metropolitan areas: Atlanta, Boston, Detroit, and Los Angeles. The firms surveyed were randomly drawn but stratified by employer size in order to generate a sample that roughly replicates the distribution of employees across firms in the workforce. Selection biases introduced by nonresponses appear to be minimal.

The data focus on a variety of employer and job characteristics. The firm-level variables include type of industry, number of employees, the existence of collective bargaining agreements, turnover, gross and net hiring, job vacancies, and hiring durations. The job-specific variables include occupation, wages and benefits paid, daily task performance on the job, recruiting and screening methods used while hiring, and some demographic characteristics of the worker hired into the last job filled by the firm.

We have used these data to analyze the locations and characteristics of employers and jobs currently available to workers without college degrees, and how these factors influence exactly who gets hired and what they are paid in these jobs. We were particularly interested in how the employment opportunities of less-educated minorities are influenced by the skill requirements, geographic locations, and racial attitudes of these employers; therefore we focused on various "mismatch" issues as well as on employer discrimination.

The major findings of this study can be summarized as follows:

- *There appears to be both a shortage of available jobs for unemployed workers in the central cities and at least some difficulty in filling jobs that are available.* While the number of jobs available is high in most of the primary central cities relative to resident populations, there is also a large net flow of suburban residents who commute in to fill those jobs. Job vacancy rates and durations are comparable or even higher in the central city than in the suburbs, partly due to higher skill requirements; but the unemployment rates of central-city residents are much higher. Thus the gaps between the numbers of unemployed workers and jobs available to residents are higher in the central city as well.
- *The vast majority of jobs available to less-educated workers are in the retail trade and service industries and are white-collar or service jobs, especially in the central cities.* Traditional blue-collar jobs, and those in industries such as construction and manufacturing, constitute only about 20–30 percent of jobs available to these workers in the metropolitan areas, and only about 20 percent or less in the central cities.
- *Most jobs available to less-educated workers require the daily performance of one or more cognitive/social tasks, such as dealing with customers, reading and writing, arithmetic calculations, and the use of computers. Many are filled through informal referrals. Most employers also require such credentials as high school diplomas, specific experience, references, and/or previous training.* Most of these job requirements are somewhat higher in the central cities than in the suburbs, even within occupational categories. Indeed, the fraction of noncollege jobs in the central city that require none of these tasks to be performed or which require none of these credentials is only about 5 percent. Most employers also seem reluctant to hire workers with unstable work histories, especially those they suspect of having criminal records.

- *Employer locations and discriminatory attitudes limit the hiring of blacks (especially males) much more than Hispanics for non-college jobs.* Blacks are roughly twice as likely to *apply* for jobs in the primary central city as in the suburbs, and black applicants are somewhat less likely to be *hired* in the suburbs as well, especially at smaller firms and where contact with white customers is involved. The latter is true despite the fact that skill needs and hiring requirements in the suburbs are *lower* than in the central cities.

  The fact that blacks primarily seek work in the central cities suggests that spatial imbalances caused by residential segregation—which is much worse in some metropolitan areas (such as Detroit) than in others—play an important role. That blacks are less likely to be hired in the suburbs suggests that racial discrimination is more severe in the suburbs. Black male applicants are the least likely to be hired of any racial or gender group.

  In contrast to these employment problems of blacks, we find little evidence that Hispanics are negatively affected by geographic location or employer discrimination at the hiring stage. Employment for Hispanics has become relatively concentrated in manufacturing and in blue-collar jobs, while employment for black males in these sectors has become quite limited; these developments appear to be only partly accounted for by the relative geographic concentration of manufacturing and blue-collar work in suburban areas.

- *Employer skill requirements appear to limit the hiring of both Hispanics and blacks for many kinds of jobs.* The hiring of both blacks and Hispanics is limited in certain types of jobs by the skill needs and credentials required by employers. Blacks are roughly twice as likely to be hired into non-college jobs that do not require any major tasks to be performed daily relative to those that do require at least some tasks; for Hispanic males the hiring rate is almost three times as high in the former as in the latter.

  Jobs that require daily computer use and arithmetic pose particular barriers to the employment of black and Hispanic males; those that require high school diplomas and customer interaction are also less available to Hispanic males, while those requiring specific experience and previous training are less available to black males. In contrast, women are relatively more likely than men within each racial group to be hired into jobs requiring the particular cognitive/interactive tasks we included in our survey, at least partly because they are heavily used in clerical and sales occupations.

- *Starting wages and benefits on jobs requiring no college are low for many workers. In general they remain highest for white males and lowest for minority females.* This is particularly true in manufacturing jobs, where wage premiums are highest for the former and virtually nonexistent for the latter. More generally, the relatively low wages of black (and Hispanic) males can largely be accounted for by the observed characteristics of workers and jobs, but this is much less true for females (especially whites).

Overall, we find that less-educated blacks and Hispanics (especially males) face their greatest difficulties at the *employment* (or hiring) stage. Black males appear to face significant barriers in the form of skill and credential requirements, as well as because of their geographic location and the discriminatory attitudes of employers. Hispanics also appear to face skill and credential barriers, but they face fewer geographic barriers and less discriminatory attitudes on the part of employers.

Limited skills and credentials also limit the *wages* available to minority males. The lower wages of white females are not so easily explained by observable factors, so we suspect that discrimination plays a relatively greater role in this case. For minority females, both sets of problems (lack of skills and credentials, and discrimination) appear to limit wages as well as employment.

POLICY IMPLICATIONS

If skills, location, and race and gender all contribute to the employment and earnings problems of minorities and females, what policies are implied by these findings?

Education, Job Training, and Work Experience

Over the long run, enhancing the job skills and credentials of minorities should be our highest priority. At the most elementary level, the high school diploma requirement remains a barrier to employment for some, especially among Hispanics. Raising high school graduation rates thus remains a critical goal. Achieving higher levels of postsecondary education among blacks and Hispanics, and even among whites, will certainly help to raise the earnings of the individuals who get such an education and should limit the competition for available jobs among those who do not.

Our analysis indicates that employers perceive a lack of a broad range of skills and credentials among black and Hispanic applicants. Improving the basic cognitive and interactive skills of minority high school graduates should therefore be an important goal of policy. Greater development of certain specific skills, such as computer literacy, would also enhance the employability of many of these workers.

However, it is also clear that blacks are particularly impaired by a general or specific lack of experience when looking for work. This implies that programs to ease the "school-to-work transition" for young blacks could have important social payoffs. Improved job placement services and better linkages between schools and employers are two means of easing the transition. But our goal should be to raise the access of high school students and graduates to meaningful private sector work experience as early as possible.

Mobility

The need to enhance job placements for young blacks raises the related question of how to improve their access to the less-skilled jobs that appear to be available in suburban areas. In answering this question one of three approaches is generally advocated: (1) Bring jobs to the city through urban development programs, by creating enterprise (or "empowerment") zones, for example; (2) bring minorities to *live* in the suburbs by means of residential mobility programs and antidiscrimination programs in housing; and (3) bring minorities to *work* in the suburbs, through programs that combine transportation and job placement assistance with training, counseling, and the like. The arguments in favor of or against each of these alternatives have been stated elsewhere at length.[1] The most cost-effective approach in the short term is probably the third, while over the longer term the first and second options each have pluses.[2]

[1] The arguments in favor of transportation/job placement approaches appear in Hughes and Sternberg (1992), while Kain (1992) argues most strongly in favor of strong antidiscrimination policies in housing as well as housing vouchers for the poor. Rosenbaum and Popkin (1991) also present evidence from the Gautreaux program in Chicago that employment rates rose when low-income adults were moved from low-income central-city areas to the suburbs. The high cost of job creation through "enterprise zones" is stressed in Papke (1992).

[2] Residential mobility for the poor not only helps them overcome "spatial mismatch" but also helps to eliminate the negative effects of living and raising children in neighborhoods segregated by race and income, as stressed by Massey and Denton (1992). But the provision of low-income housing in the suburbs often faces strong political opposition, and "white flight" from integrating suburbs often undercuts the goals of removing discrimination in housing markets. Arguments for "enterprise zones" must rest on the long-term benefits of revitalizing communities and commercial areas and the potential spillovers from early economic development.

Whichever approach is taken, improving the access of inner-city minorities to suburban employers could have high payoffs, given the magnitudes of the differentials in applicant rates that currently exist across geographic areas.

Federal Antidiscrimination Policy

It appears that employer discrimination against blacks is more pervasive in smaller establishments and in the suburbs more than in the central cities. Indeed, it is likely that more discriminatory employers choose to locate in areas that are as far away as possible from minority residential populations, thus deliberately choosing to lower minority access to their firms (and perhaps their own exposure to equal employment opportunity litigation as well).

It might be useful to target those suburban firms that get significant numbers of minority applicants but hire a smaller percentage of them than their central-city counterparts do for greater EEO enforcement.[3] But since many firms in the suburbs receive few such applicants, improving the access of central-city residents to these suburban firms remains a prerequisite of any such direct pressure on the demand side of the market. Indeed, mobility programs on the supply side and antidiscrimination efforts on the demand side, both targeting major suburban employers, could be viewed as complementary approaches to improving employment opportunities for inner-city residents.

As for the *wage* discrimination that women appear to face, some analysts (for example, Sorensen 1994) advocate "comparable worth" policies to raise the rewards associated with the performance of jobs that are predominantly female. But given the questions that remain about the supply-versus-demand causes of these differentials as well as potential employment losses from the "comparable worth" approach, enhanced enforcement of current EEO laws would be a more cautious but probably more prudent approach.

[3]For a review of recent history and evidence on the employment effects of EEO enforcement and affirmative action, see Leonard (1990). For a skeptical view on the potential benefits of greater EEO enforcement, see Bloch (1994).

Job Creation

A strong implication of our findings presented in chapter 3 is that for the least-skilled, least-educated, and least-experienced members of our society there appear to be a very limited number of jobs available in the short term. This looks to be true for those at the "back of the queue" for hiring even when the overall level of job availability appears fairly strong (though these individuals are relatively better off when job markets are tight). Furthermore, if long-term AFDC recipients are required to enter the workforce in substantial numbers, the imbalance between job availability and the numbers of low-skill workers will no doubt worsen.

Thus, while other options (such as enhanced education and training) certainly have the greatest appeal for the longer term, there is probably no alternative to some direct job creation for very unskilled workers in the short term.

The most cost-effective approach, often favored by economists, would be to target wage subsidies on employers of disadvantaged workers. There are some questions about whether such subsidies result in any *net* job creation or just the substitution of subsidized for unsubsidized workers.[4] More important, it is possible that the stigma created by the subsidy itself outweighs the attractiveness of the subsidy, making the entire effort counterproductive.[5]

While other approaches to subsidized private-sector job creation should be explored, at least some direct job creation through public service employment will likely be necessary.[6] While minimum-wage jobs in the current environment are of very limited appeal to many workers, it appears that a significant fraction of currently nonemployed individuals would be willing to accept

[4]See, for instance, Bishop (1993) for evidence on the Targeted Job Tax Credit.

[5]See Burtless (1985) and Hollenbeck and Willke (1991). Because of these problems with targeted subsidies or credits, some economists (see Haveman 1988) prefer a return to a marginal employment tax credit (such as the New Jobs Tax Credit of the late 1970s) that would pay firms only if they generate *net* new employment (above some base level from the previous year) and would cap the dollar level of hourly wages for which the credit is available, thereby providing higher subsidies for low-wage workers in percentage terms.

[6]See Danziger and Gottschalk (1995) for strong arguments in favor of public service employment. Lehman (1994) presents interesting arguments for wage subsidies targeted on all residents of low-income areas rather than on only the most disadvantaged or only those who work in "enterprise zones."

them.[7] If AFDC recipients are required to obtain work, the number willing to accept such work would surely grow even further.

Improving the Rewards to Work

Despite the relatively high task-performance and hiring criteria observed in many non-college jobs, we demonstrated in chapter 2 that there are a substantial number of such jobs that pay relatively little. These limited rewards have been linked to declining labor force participation and increased criminal activity among young males, especially minorities.[8] Unlike AFDC recipients, there is little in the way of direct work requirements that can be imposed on such individuals.

Improving the perceived returns to low-wage employment must therefore remain a priority. The dramatic 1993 expansion of the Earned Income Tax Credit by the Clinton administration needs to be preserved and built upon. Improving the means of informing those who are eligible for this credit, expanding eligibility to some of those who are not covered currently (such as some single individuals), and providing other benefits (such as health care) to low-income individuals and families are additional steps that should be considered over time.[9] Increasing the federal minimum wage would also increase the perceived returns to work.[10]

THE NEED FOR FURTHER RESEARCH

The data presented in this volume provide some fairly striking empirical facts about the number and nature of available jobs for less-skilled workers. But many of these findings are open to interpretations other than the ones we have offered. Nor have we conclusively proven the hypotheses described in chapter 1.

[7] In the Detroit Area Survey, about 20 percent of nonemployed black young adults claimed that they would accept work at $4.00 per hour, while roughly 50 percent would accept it at $5.00. Among AFDC recipients, the reported reservation wages were even lower.

[8] See Juhn (1992) and Freeman (1994).

[9] See Danziger and Gottschalk (1995).

[10] Whether the minimum wage has any significant disemployment effects has once again become the subject of some controversy recently. For two opposing views, see Card and Krueger (1994), and Neumark and Wascher (1992).

A clearer set of comparisons is necessary between the demand-side data and the data on workers from the supply side of the market. In further work with these data, we hope to link individual workers and firms for the firms sampled directly from the household survey and to link households with subsets of firms that are either geographically nearby or that appear "matchable" in terms of employer criteria and personal characteristics.

The extent to which the characteristics of such firms help to explain the *variance* in employment and earnings outcomes across individuals can thereby be more fully explored.[11] The geographic matching, in particular, should enable us to more fully explore "spatial mismatch" issues, by analyzing the extent to which nearby (as opposed to metropolitan-wide) job availability and characteristics affect employment outcomes of individuals.

A variety of other hypotheses that we explored here remain open to question. In particular, sorting out the legitimate effects of employer skill requirements and worker deficiencies from the effects of employer discrimination remains difficult. On the one hand, differences in hiring rates of minorities across firms and geographic areas may be caused by unobserved differences in those employers or in the characteristics of workers who apply to them; in such cases, what appears to be discriminatory behavior may really be prudent screening. On the other hand, *perceived* differences in worker abilities may not be real, or they may not be terribly relevant to worker performance; in such cases, what appear to be legitimate skill needs of employers may turn out to be discriminatory attitudes and perceptions on their part.

Other approaches that also focus on the demand side of the labor market may help to shed more light here. The audit studies of employers discussed in chapter 4 (for example, Fix and Struyk 1993) have controlled more carefully for personal characteristics and thus provide clearer evidence of discriminatory differences in hiring.[12] More qualitative studies of employers and their workers

[11] Plans to perform such analyses are already part of the Multi-City Study of Urban Inequality, of which this survey was a part. Geographic matching of our firms and households can be done since all firms and households have been "geocoded" through Geographic Information Systems and matched to census tracts and block groups.

[12] Even the results of audit studies are plagued by the problem of employers who apparently believe that there are *unobserved* differences across job applicants by race

will also give us better insights into the attitudes and experiences of the employers in dealing with workers.[13]

There is also a need to assess the extent to which observable differences by race or gender in cognitive abilities or other personal characteristics really affect worker performance and therefore the employment and earnings of different groups of workers. Such studies are very difficult to undertake, since objective measures of performance are hard to come by; even where they exist, they would surely differ across industries and firms. Furthermore, any studies of worker performance will be subject to serious selection biases caused by employer hiring policies.[14]

Nevertheless, the relationships between *signals* of productivity that are observed prior to hiring and the levels of productivity that are observed after hiring are critical to any true understanding of the issues analyzed here. Ultimately, we hope to see this relationship explored more fully.

who appear to be observationally equivalent across a few dimensions. The audits thus give us no insight into real differences in the quantity or quality of labor supply from different groups facing any given set of firms. Perhaps a new generation of such studies will ultimately focus on the broader issues of how job applicants are matched to firms in a given labor market.

[13] Ongoing work by Katherine Newman and Carol Stack at McDonald's establishments in Oakland and Harlem, and also by Joleen Kirschenman, Phil Moss, and Chris Tilly in the same four metropolitan areas that I have studied, should be very useful.

[14] In general, more significant employer screens against minorities will bias any results for *hired* employees toward equality across groups.

Appendix A: An Analysis of Survey Response Rates

Here we consider the extent to which our sample of firms may suffer from sample selection bias.

We have analyzed the fractions of firms that successfully completed our screening (which we refer to as "screening rates") and the fractions of these screened firms that successfully completed our survey (which we refer to as "response rates"). We compare these rates across categories of variables observable for all firms (that is, those that did not complete the screening or that did not respond as well as those that did) to discover any selection bias across these observable categories.[1]

In order to successfully complete the screening, we first needed to establish contact with an employee at a firm and then contact the individual responsible for hiring. The firms generated by SSI had to have hired someone into a position not requiring a college diploma and the firms generated by the household surveys had to have hired someone into a specified occupational category during the previous three years.

We grouped firms that did not successfully complete the survey according to the reasons for their nonparticipation, which included refusals, "incapables" (due to language difficulties, for example), and persistent no-answers or busy signals. In at least some of these cases, it was not clear whether a firm should be listed as a nonresponse. Therefore, we calculated the response rates in two different ways: (1) only refusals and incapables were listed as nonresponses; and (2) persistent no-answers and busy signals were added to the previous category. These response rates are referred to as "R-1" and "R-2," respectively, in table A.1; the corresponding screening rates are referred to as "S-1" and "S-2."[2] The various screening and response rates are presented by metropolitan area and by household versus SSI sample.

[1] We were also concerned about nonrandom selection on the basis of *un*observed characteristics, though we can say very little about this directly. Therefore, we used differences across the observed categories for making inferences about both.

[2] In other words, where "no-answers" are not included among the nonresponses, they are included among the firms that failed to complete the screening.

Table A.1 / Response and Screen Rates by Metropolitan Area and Data Source

	Response Rates		Screening Rates	
	R-1[a]	R-2[b]	S-1[c]	S-2[d]
Total	.682	.665	.702	.717
	(.007)	(.007)	(.005)	(.004)
By Metropolitan Area				
Atlanta	.674	.671	.725	.731
	(.014)	(.014)	(.009)	(.009)
Boston	.646	.644	.697	.711
	(.014)	(.014)	(.009)	(.008)
Los Angeles	.660	.657	.632	.649
	(.014)	(.014)	(.009)	(.009)
Detroit	.760	.688	.771	.793
	(.013)	(.014)	(.009)	(.009)
By Sample				
Household	.737	.692	.826	.840
	(.012)	(.012)	(.007)	(.007)
SSI	.660	.653	.660	.675
	(.008)	(.008)	(.005)	(.005)
Detroit				
Household	.763	.663	.862	.871
	(.018)	(.019)	(.010)	(.010)
SSI	.756	.720	.678	.714
	(.019)	(.020)	(.014)	(.014)
Other Areas				
Household	.719	.715	.800	.818
	(.016)	(.016)	(.010)	(.010)
SSI	.643	.641	.657	.668
	(.009)	(.009)	(.006)	(.006)

NOTE: Standard errors of means are in parentheses.
[a] Only refusals and "incapables" are listed as nonresponses.
[b] Persistent no-answers and busy signals are added to the nonresponse category.
[c] Firms in the above two categories are included among those who failed to complete the screening.
[d] Firms in the above two categories are not included among those who failed to complete the screening.

The results of the data show that roughly 70 percent of all firms whose names we received were successfully screened and that 67–68 percent of these responded to the interviews with completed surveys.

We note that the screening rates were somewhat lower in Los Angeles than elsewhere. Since our survey period began within a year of serious racial disturbances in Los Angeles, and since the 1994 earthquake occurred during the survey period, this is not surprising.[3]

We also note that response rates in Detroit were somewhat higher than elsewhere.[4] But the differentials between Detroit and the other metropolitan areas are never larger than 10 percentage points in magnitude.

Interestingly, firms generated by respondents to the household survey had both higher screening rates and response rates than those generated by SSI. The higher screening rates of the former may reflect the greater tendency of employees to generate names of firms in which they are currently working and remain open in the metropolitan areas. On the other hand, significant fractions of eligible individuals from the household surveys failed to report firms at all (which is not reflected in the screening rates),[5] thus rendering the overall rates at which firms were generated from the two sources more comparable. The explanations for the higher response rates among screened firms from the household samples (accounted for almost totally by firms from areas other than Detroit) are not clear, but, again, the differences in magnitude are not very large.

In table A.2 we test for significant differences in response and screening rates ("R-2" and "S-2," respectively) across firm characteristics that were available even for nonrespondents and non-

[3]There are many reports of firms leaving the Los Angeles area in response to the riots of 1992, which would be reflected in a lower screening rate. However, we could not confirm that this was in fact the cause of the lower rates observed here.

[4]Many interviewers attributed the higher response rate (when more narrowly defined) in Detroit to its proximity to Michigan State University and to the frequency with which respondent individuals were alumni.

[5]This was substantially more true among the currently unemployed than among the employed, but it was also somewhat more true among blacks and central-city residents than among other household respondents. More details are available from the author.

Table A.2 / Response and Screen Rates by Firm Characteristics

	R-2	S-2
Location		
Suburbs	.680	—
	(.011)	
Primary Central City	.654	—
	(.016)	
Other	.659	—
	(.022)	
Size (number of employees)		
1–19	.645	.533
	(.018)	(.012)
20–99	.675	.604
	(.012)	(.009)
100+	.682	.766
	(.014)	(.010)
Industry		
Construction	.587	.519
	(.057)	(.037)
Manufacturing	.678	.672
	(.017)	(.013)
T.C.U.[a]	.655	.600
	(.034)	(.024)
Wholesale Trade	.668	.563
	(.024)	(.018)
Retail Trade	.665	.672
	(.020)	(.015)
F.I.R.E.[b]	.647	.615
	(.026)	(.019)
Services	.682	.618
	(.015)	(.011)
Public	.773	.720
	(.091)	(.064)

NOTE: These rates are computed for SSI firms only. Nonscreened firms had not yet been categorized by location at the time of the analysis, so screening rates are not computed by location here.
[a] Transportation, Communication, and Utilities.
[b] Finance, Insurance, and Real Estate.

screened firms in the SSI data. From any differences we find in response rates across observable characteristics, we can infer the extent to which selection bias from nonrandomly distributed nonresponses might be a problem. The observed characteristics included location within the metropolitan area, established size, and broad industry category.

In general, the results show few significant differences in response rates across these categories of firms, and even where the differences are significant, they are often not terribly large. Response rates rise by small amounts as firm size increases; in many cases, it was easier to identify the relevant individuals within personnel departments of larger companies, and their willingness to be surveyed seemed greater as well. Excluding construction and the public sector (both of which represent fairly small fractions of the overall industrial distribution discussed in chapter 2), response rates vary quite little across industries or across locations within the metropolitan area.

The tendency to pass the screening process rises significantly with firm size, but this is surely to be expected: smaller firms are a good deal more likely to go out of business than are larger ones (Brown, Hamilton, and Medoff 1990). The differentials between successful screening rates across industries also vary more than do the response rates, no doubt reflecting differences in firm stability as well as in the tendencies of firms to have hired in recent years.

Finally, we also compared distributions of firms in our completed samples to those observed for each metropolitan area in the Bureau of Labor Statistics' *County Business Patterns,* and we compared distributions of occupations reported among last-hired workers to those observed in the published summaries of the 1990 Census for each area. More detail on these comparisons is presented in chapter 2, but overall we found the industrial and occupational distributions here to be quite comparable to those found by the Bureau of Labor Statistics and the Census Bureau.

Thus, we conclude that employer nonresponses are fairly randomly distributed in this survey and that selection bias from nonrandom response does not seriously impair the data we have collected.

Appendix B: Additional Tables for Chapter 2

Table B.1 / Establishment Size by Location

	Atlanta			Boston			Detroit			Los Angeles		
	PCC[a]	SUB[b]	OTH[c]	PCC	SUB	OTH	PCC	SUB	OTH	PCC	SUB	OTH
Mean Employment												
Regular	495.0	156.7	317.8	405.8	261.7	257.1	1252.6	384.7	364.7	230.2	228.8	1783.1
Temporary	54.6	4.7	11.2	29.0	6.4	5.7	8.6	10.9	19.3	9.3	15.2	18.6
Contracted	26.8	2.3	37.3	6.9	5.0	13.0	20.8	8.3	9.1	8.0	8.5	70.1
Total	547.8	167.7	366.6	441.7	273.2	275.7	1281.7	403.9	393.3	247.7	252.7	1872.0
Median Employment												
Regular	50	37	41	50	34	60	54	41	46	50	53	100
Total	51	37	50	54	39	62	70	45	46	51	60	106
Firms with Total Employment												
<25	.327	.382	.333	.394	.399	.311	.348	.356	.354	.335	.295	.276
≥25, <100	.284	.321	.273	.251	.241	.299	.202	.290	.286	.250	.285	.218
≥100, <1000	.290	.251	.355	.344	.288	.297	.268	.290	.247	.276	.366	.318
≥1000	.099	.046	.039	.111	.062	.093	.182	.064	.113	.039	.054	.188

[a]Primary central city.
[b]Suburbs
[c]Other areas, as defined in table 2.2.

Table B.2 / Establishment Size by Industry and Location

	Manufacturing			Retail Trade			Services		
	PCC[a]	SUB[b]	OTH[c]	PCC	SUB	OTH	PCC	SUB	OTH
Mean Employment									
Regular	199.2	228.0	398.1	65.9	158.4	89.5	777.2	345.8	1027.1
Temporary	3.8	7.6	8.8	1.2	1.5	3.1	39.1	17.8	20.1
Contracted	1.7	5.2	6.4	1.7	2.7	1.1	10.6	66.4	63.2
Total	204.7	240.8	413.3	68.9	162.5	93.7	827.6	372.0	1111.7
Median Employment									
Regular	64	80	95	23	35	50	89	42	65
Total	65	90	100	23	36	50	100	45	65
Firms with Total Employment									
<25	.278	.223	.284	.520	.404	.345	.262	.381	.276
≥25, <100	.318	.320	.215	.269	.332	.379	.237	.221	.313
≥100, <1000	.372	.408	.436	.209	.248	.276	.367	.316	.239
≥1000	.032	.049	.065	.002	.016	.000	.134	.082	.172

[a]Primary central city.
[b]Suburbs.
[c]Other areas, as defined in table 2.2.

Table B.3 / Gross and Net Hiring, Turnover, and Vacancies

A. Means (standard deviation)	
Gross Hire Rate	.257 (.546)
Turnover Rate	
Quits	.143 (.249)
Discharges	.068 (.129)
Net Hire Rate	
Reported	.080 (.433)
Implied	.013 (.498)
Vacancy Rate	.027 (.069)

B. Correlations Across Rates

	Gross Hire	Quit	Discharge	Net Hire (Reported)	Net Hire (Implied)	Vacancy
Gross Hire	—	.612	.457	.102	.081	.127
Quit	—	—	.320	.030	.001	.215
Discharge	—	—	—	.079	−.075	.188
Net Hiring (Reported)	—	—	—	—	.327	.071
Net Hiring (Implied)	—	—	—	—	—	−.024
Vacancy	—	—	—	—	—	—

NOTE: "Reported" and "Implied" net hire rates are defined in the text.

Table B.4 / Hire, Turnover, and Vacancy Rates by Industry and Location

	Manufacturing			Retail Trade			Services		
	PCC[a]	SUB[b]	OTH[c]	PCC	SUB	OTH	PCC	SUB	OTH
Gross Hire Rate	.130	.160	.169	.228	.216	.257	.231	.295	.377
Turnover Rates									
Quits	.058	.074	.077	.169	.141	.122	.114	.125	.207
Discharges	.044	.093	.104	.070	.076	.064	.060	.062	.099
Job Vacancy Rate	.020	.019	.013	.037	.033	.058	.026	.027	.027

[a]Primary central city.
[b]Suburbs
[c]Other areas, as defined in table 2.2.

Table B.5 / Wages and Benefits by Industry and Location

	Manufacturing			Retail Trade			Services		
	PCC[a]	SUB[b]	OTH[c]	PCC	SUB	OTH	PCC	SUB	OTH
No College Required									
Weekly Wage									
Mean	330.78	386.34	353.60	257.92	202.05	178.28	344.49	308.32	300.78
(S.D.)	(137.99)	(165.54)	(172.30)	(126.82)	(145.52)	(101.34)	(145.64)	(156.40)	(140.18)
Median	400	315	360	288	300	280	385	300	310
Hourly Wage									
Mean	8.16	9.02	8.75	6.72	6.06	5.43	9.25	8.84	8.39
(S.D.)	(3.18)	(3.61)	(3.67)	(2.41)	(2.72)	(2.16)	(3.65)	13.31	(3.81)
Median	10.00	7.69	9.00	7.00	7.00	8.00	9.87	8.00	8.00
Hourly Wages $6.00 or Less	.000	.275	.157	.440	.340	.214	.086	.174	.094
Benefits									
Own Health Insurance	.813	.912	.891	.679	.587	.600	.806	.713	.769
Family Health Insurance	.733	.839	.827	.449	.504	.468	.679	.605	.635
Employer Contribution to Pension	.344	.617	.685	.431	.420	.474	.589	.432	.564

[a]Primary central city.
[b]Suburbs.
[c]Other areas, as defined in table 2.2.

Appendix C: Additional Tables for Chapter 4

Table C.1 / Race and Gender of New Hires among Young or Less-Educated Workers

	Atlanta			Boston		
	PCC[a]	SUB[b]	OTH[c]	PCC	SUB	OTH
No College Required						
Males						
White	.170	.310	.327	.272	.405	.245
Black	.206	.131	.178	.090	.047	.034
Hispanic	.009	.030	.016	.029	.039	.176
Females						
White	.354	.374	.301	.468	.428	.317
Black	.221	.123	.136	.058	.016	.086
Hispanic	.020	.008	.019	.065	.026	.124
High School or Less						
Males						
White	.140	.326	.370	.357	.462	.258
Black	.293	.190	.201	.107	.066	.024
Hispanic	.013	.013	.023	.023	.038	.227
Females						
White	.248	.304	.255	.331	.347	.222
Black	.254	.138	.100	.076	.016	.107
Hispanic	.038	.006	.016	.104	.029	.163
Ages 16–34, No College Required						
Males						
White	.180	.278	.302	.239	.404	.226
Black	.197	.188	.247	.086	.054	.027
Hispanic	.014	.043	.012	.008	.043	.226
Females						
White	.331	.320	.289	.492	.407	.307
Black	.232	.136	.123	.060	.020	.124
Hispanic	.024	.006	.028	.086	.031	.063
Ages 16–34, High School or Less						
Males						
White	.159	.317	.389	.385	.483	.273
Black	.292	.255	.264	.089	.072	.020
Hispanic	.018	.020	.016	.000	.037	.301
Females						
White	.197	.261	.223	.317	.307	.174
Black	.272	.130	.087	.089	.024	.160
Hispanic	.043	.000	.021	.117	.030	.072

NOTE: The numbers for each of the four main categories sum to approximately one vertically.
[a] Primary central city.
[b] Suburbs.
[c] Other areas, as defined in table 2.2.

	Detroit			Los Angeles		
	PCC	SUB	OTH	PCC	SUB	OTH
No College Required						
Males						
White	.198	.350	.267	.078	.152	.171
Black	.224	.062	.161	.056	.040	.141
Hispanic	.010	.021	.022	.308	.226	.195
Females						
White	.198	.449	.373	.144	.240	.227
Black	.341	.094	.153	.063	.064	.040
Hispanic	.019	.007	.011	.168	.198	.122
High School or Less						
Males						
White	.127	.393	.212	.033	.072	.126
Black	.275	.059	.168	.044	.050	.101
Hispanic	.016	.036	.043	.480	.289	.283
Females						
White	.193	.392	.357	.083	.220	.271
Black	.342	.086	.213	.102	.051	.000
Hispanic	.031	.005	.000	.176	.262	.189
Ages 16–34, No College Required						
Males						
White	.138	.331	.235	.073	.144	.143
Black	.270	.081	.161	.054	.029	.121
Hispanic	.015	.028	.037	.340	.256	.210
Females						
White	.194	.443	.340	.112	.195	.283
Black	.368	.110	.185	.063	.082	.034
Hispanic	.015	.007	.018	.236	.233	.093
Ages 16–34, High School or Less						
Males						
White	.115	.417	.300	.031	.072	.138
Black	.303	.086	.186	.031	.037	.147
Hispanic	.022	.050	.068	.509	.297	.321
Females						
White	.158	.363	.170	.020	.193	.257
Black	.381	.084	.265	.077	.069	.000
Hispanic	.022	.000	.000	.249	.290	.138

Table C.2. / Occupation/Industry of New Hires for Non-College Jobs by Race, Gender, and Location

	Occupation							
	Atlanta				Boston			
	PM[a]	SC[b]	CO[c]	LS[d]	PM	SC	CO	LS
Males								
White	.157	.357	.316	.164	.093	.332	.360	.215
Black	.044	.353	.287	.298	.094	.349	.252	.305
Hispanic	.058	.070	.269	.604	.065	.307	.410	.218
Females								
White	.188	.657	.052	.104	.243	.604	.055	.084
Black	.104	.601	.135	.161	.088	.802	.000	.110
Hispanic	.123	.761	.000	.116	.023	.468	.406	.102

	Industry					
	Atlanta			Boston		
	MFG[e]	RT[f]	S[g]	MFG	RT	S
Males						
White	.221	.176	.234	.328	.203	.254
Black	.224	.264	.222	.158	.097	.494
Hispanic	.329	.000	.162	.527	.091	.228
Females						
White	.178	.137	.402	.161	.159	.393
Black	.178	.248	.349	.047	.001	.728
Hispanic	.101	.280	.597	.457	.068	.258

NOTE: Occupations sum to approximately one *horizontally* for each metropolitan area, while industries sum to less than one.
[a] Professional/managerial.
[b] Sales/clerical.
[c] Crafts/operative.
[d] Laborer/service.
[e] Manufacturing.
[f] Retail/trade.
[g] Services.

	Occupation							
	Detroit				Los Angeles			
	PM	SC	CO	LS	PM	SC	CO	LS
Males								
White	.150	.191	.434	.211	217	349	.287	.123
Black	.069	.165	.389	.377	.082	.272	.251	.395
Hispanic	.085	.169	.662	.085	.082	.218	.451	.243
Females								
White	.180	.593	.063	.156	.138	.774	.038	.050
Black	.117	.512	.074	.298	.134	.724	.005	.137
Hispanic	.000	.500	.000	.500	.088	.629	.131	.152

	Industry					
	Detroit			Los Angeles		
	MFG	RT	S	MFG	RT	S
Males						
White	.318	.161	.215	.276	.162	.302
Black	.190	.242	.314	.174	.112	.400
Hispanic	.352	.203	.343	.443	.139	.249
Females						
White	.104	.231	.365	.204	.154	.383
Black	.103	.263	.417	.030	.293	.315
Hispanic	.000	.600	.400	.164	.161	.500

Table C.3. / Race and Gender of New Hires for Non-College Jobs by Occupation/Industry and Location

	Atlanta		Boston		Detroit		Los Angeles	
	PCC[a]	SUB[b]	PCC	SUB	PCC	SUB	PCC	SUB
Sales/Clerical								
Males								
White	.137	.214	.281	.273	.130	.167	.064	.114
Black	.119	.083	.075	.033	.148	.023	.055	.010
Hispanic	.005	.000	.000	.017	.000	.000	.157	.084
Females								
White	.440	.553	.465	.590	.323	.653	.205	.376
Black	.253	.130	.071	.028	.366	.122	.094	.094
Hispanic	.026	.019	.071	.045	.033	.012	.225	.237
Craft/Operative								
Males								
White	.349	.466	.553	.654	.530	.603	.087	.190
Black	.433	.243	.012	.074	.309	.139	.058	.062
Hispanic	.000	.033	.108	.075	.045	.059	.581	.514
Females								
White	.035	.131	.108	.116	.045	.143	.008	.055
Black	.183	.127	.000	.000	.072	.047	.000	.000
Hispanic	.000	.000	.215	.011	.000	.000	.087	.116
Manufacturing								
Males								
White	.187	.322	.406	.541	.185	.571	.131	.149
Black	.212	.157	.000	.039	.431	.060	.000	.051
Hispanic	.033	.027	.000	.068	.000	.039	.575	.378
Females								
White	.404	.293	.396	.269	.105	.247	.059	.194
Black	.133	.153	.000	.010	.278	.061	.000	.008
Hispanic	.033	.000	.198	.010	.000	.000	.105	.128
Service								
Males								
White	.151	.224	.188	.326	.157	.254	.041	.135
Black	.091	.055	.157	.051	.178	.053	.053	.043
Hispanic	.009	.017	.053	.036	.000	.030	.197	.156
Females								
White	.436	.511	.451	.525	.223	.547	.148	.275
Black	.251	.143	.086	.009	.421	.104	.058	.045
Hispanic	.029	.033	.063	.027	.022	.000	.215	.273

NOTE: The numbers sum vertically to one within each location and occupational/industry group.
[a] Primary central city.
[b] Suburbs.

Table C.4 / Black Applicant and Hire Rates for Non-College Jobs by Industry and Location

	Constr.	Mfg.	Transp., Comm., and Util.	Wholesale Trade	Retail Trade	Finance, Ins., and R. Estate	Services	Public Sector
Primary Central Cities								
% Apps.,[a] Black Males	.424	.220	.267	.231	.314	.120	.177	.359
Ratio, Employees to Apps.	.307	.673	.745	.576	.567	.573	.808	.573
Ratio, Hires to Apps.	.376	.612	.905	.593	.856	.437	.520	.691
% Apps., Black Females	.092	.113	.136	.064	.246	.188	.214	.200
Ratio, Employees to Apps.	.557	.699	.808	.880	.732	1.170	1.033	1.218
Ratio, Hires to Apps.	.000	.596	.411	.787	.764	1.070	.725	1.750
Suburbs								
% Apps., Black Males	.142	.117	.185	.143	.144	.081	.089	.91
Ratio, Employees to Apps.	.732	.786	.378	.371	.493	.371	.495	.563
Ratio, Hires to Apps.	.738	.585	.754	.324	.463	.399	.371	.407
% Apps., Black Females	.015	.074	.096	.093	.112	.096	.092	.071
Ratio, Employee to Apps.	.921	.805	.419	.250	.496	.634	.638	.853
Ratio, Hires to Apps.	.000	.564	.970	.390	.852	.519	.473	2.211

[a] Applicants.

Table C.5 / Black Applicant and Hire Rates for Non-College Jobs by Occupation and Location

	Prof./Mgt.	Sales	Clerical	Crafts	Operative	Laborer	Service
Primary Central Cities							
% Apps.,[a] Black Males	.123	.184	.186	.249	.377	.335	.314
Ratio, Hires to Apps.	.532	.812	.384	.681	.688	1.074	.923
% Apps., Black Females	.194	.174	.204	.109	.076	.093	.262
Ratio, Hires to Apps.	.305	.683	.987	.953	.680	1.014	1.120
Suburbs							
% Apps., Black Males	.076	.144	.098	.097	.157	.189	.133
Ratio, Hires to Apps.	.462	.251	.199	.871	.855	.766	.587
% Apps., Black Females	.093	.106	.095	.027	.083	.072	.112
Ratio, Hires to Apps.	.408	.783	.757	.904	.495	.187	.681

[a] Applicants.

Table C.6 / Logit Estimates for Determinants of Hiring for Non-College Jobs: Coefficients (and Standard Errors)

	White Males				Black Males			
	1	2	3	4	1	2	3	4
Tasks (Daily)								
Customers	−.544**	−.436**	−.245**	−.172	−.275**	−.063	−.199	−.444*
	(.105)	(.122)	(.148)	(.203)	(.146)	(.170)	(.204)	(.298)
Read/Write	.173**	.204**	.254**	.035	−.111	−.057	−.117	.035
	(.103)	(.111)	(.122)	(.159)	(.141)	(.150)	(.166)	(.234)
Arithmetic	.429**	.394**	.259**	.211*	−.507**	−.440**	−.537**	−.513*
	(.105)	(.110)	(.123)	(.164)	(.139)	(.146)	(.164)	(.241)
Computers	−.777**	−.706**	−.353**	−.212	−.607**	−.475**	−.092	−.057
	(.105)	(.113)	(.132)	(.173)	(.151)	(.161)	(.192)	(.271)
Recruiting Method								
Help-Wanted Sign	—	−.569**	−.729**	−.636**	—	−.368	−.579	−.912*
		(.283)	(.314)	(.378)		(.423)	(.466)	(.623)
Newspaper Ad	—	−.550**	−.465**	−.724**	—	.125	.181	.121
		(.143)	(.161)	(.218)		(.226)	(.251)	(.368)
Walk-in	—	−.555**	−.522**	−.493**	—	.221	−.002	−.302
		(.174)	(.193)	(.254)		(.239)	(.268)	(.395)
Current employee	—	−.485**	−.479**	−.595**	—	−.043	−.034	.063
		(.147)	(.163)	(.215)		(.226)	(.247)	(.343)
State Emp. Serv.	—	−.803**	−.742**	−.166	—	.908**	1.022**	.908*
		(.300)	(.326)	(.437)		(.342)	(.377)	(.623)
Pvt. Emp. Serv	—	−1.015**	−.831**	−.605*	—	.029	−.098	−.395
		(.285)	(.305)	(.460)		(.356)	(.426)	(.786)
Com. Agency	—	−.726**	−.821**	−1.328	—	.722*	.573	−.786
		(.441)	(.493)	(1.083)		(.478)	(.555)	(1.223)
School	—	−.103	.027	.083	—	−.016	.244	−.024
		(.267)	(.293)	(.395)		(.446)	(.475)	(.730)
Union	—	.076	−.550	.215	—	−.562	−.371	−.024
		(.530)	(.653)	(.968)		(1.160)	(1.098)	(.730)
Affirmative Action	—	−.358**	−.243**	−.131	—	.101	.049	−.115
		(.103)	(.115)	(.154)		(.147)	(.165)	(.235)
Require								
High School Diploma	—	−.077	.176	.169	—	−.091	−.018	−.095
		(.125)	(.139)	(.182)		(.168)	(.186)	(.265)
General Experience	—	.136	.070	.296*	—	−.057	−.029	−.128
		(.122)	(.132)	(.180)		(.165)	(.181)	(.262)
Specific Experience	—	.143	.120	−.152	—	−.166	−.134	−.006
		(.121)	(.134)	(.180)		(.165)	(.183)	(.267)
Voc. Ed. or Training	—	.238**	.196*	.170	—	−.204	−.130	−.191
		(.113)	(.123)	(.170)		(.165)	(.184)	(.266)
References	—	.017	.018	.104	—	.019	.019	−.125
		(.118)	(.130)	(.177)		(.162)	(.180)	(.265)

NOTE: Dependent variable is a dichotous variable indicating whether last employee hired was a member of the particular race/gender group. One asterisk indicates significance at only the .20 level in a two-tailed test, and two asterisks indicate at least .10 significance. The omitted category for recruitment dummies is other referrals, while for firm-size dummies it is those with more than 500 employees.

	White Females				Black Females			
	1	2	3	4	1	2	3	4
Tasks (Daily)								
Customers	−.953**	.746**	.468**	.690**	.759**	.561**	.414**	−.200
	(.116)	(.132)	(.153)	(.226)	(.168)	(.188)	(.213)	(.351)
Read/Write	−.131*	−.285**	−.295**	−.375**	−.238**	−.201*	−.336**	.038
	(.099)	(.107)	(.122)	(.163)	(.135)	(.144)	(.161)	(.233)
Arithmetic	.080	.079	.216**	.225*	−.501**	−.518**	−.299**	−.286
	(.100)	(.107)	(.121)	(.167)	(.135)	(.141)	(.158)	(.335)
Computers	1.050**	.865**	.419**	.387**	.402**	.394**	.332**	.648**
	(.100)	(.108)	(.129)	(.174)	(.139)	(.148)	(.175)	(.256)
Recruiting Method								
Help-Wanted Sign	—	.155	.394*	.614**	—	.778**	.768**	.709*
		(.255)	(.279)	(.348)		(.309)	(.338)	(.463)
Newspaper Ad	—	.612**	.575**	.784**	—	.043	−.020	.093
		(.143)	(.161)	(.217)		(.218)	(.240)	(.358)
Walk-in	—	−.105	.043	.063	—	.692**	.734**	.765**
		(.178)	(.199)	(.268)		(.223)	(.248)	(.371)
Current employee	—	.235**	.308**	.528**	—	.050	.124	.077
		(.151)	(.169)	(.277)		(.219)	(.241)	(.355)
State Emp. Serv.	—	−.334	−.396	−.244	—	.452	.599*	−.194
		(.329)	(.370)	(.537)		(.405)	(.447)	(.844)
Pvt. Emp. Serv	—	.927**	.916**	−.918**	—	.307	.572**	.853**
		(.237)	(.266)	(.412)		(.332)	(.362)	(.584)
Com. Agency	—	−1.793**	−1.88**	−1.753*	—	.325	.487	1.434*
		(.753)	(.782)	(1.144)		(.545)	(.610)	(.984)
School	—	−.211	−.361	−.522	—	.505*	.498*	.627
		(.265)	(.304)	(.451)		(.340)	(.375)	(.556)
Union	—	−.092	.352	−.309	—	−.588	−.160	−.176
		(.640)	(.701)	(1.220)		(1.067)	(1.125)	(1.008)
Affirmative Action	—	.111	.099	.099	—	−.020	−.228*	−.511**
		(.102)	(.116)	(.157)		(.141)	(.156)	(.223)
Require								
High School Diploma	—	.360**	.057	−.030	—	.199	.189	.435**
		(.131)	(.149)	(.197)		(.175)	(.198)	(.284)
General Experience	—	.175*	.207*	.060	—	−.269**	−.246**	−.259
		(.121)	(.134)	(.183)		(.160)	(.175)	(.256)
Specific Experience	—	−.112	−.066	.082	—	−.029	−.046	−.190
		(.116)	(.130)	(.172)		(.157)	(.172)	(.256)
Voc. Ed. or Training	—	−.125	−.132	−.120	—	−.250*	−.162	−.029
		(.108)	(.122)	(.170)		(.154)	(.168)	(.251)
References	—	.012	.048	−.040	—	.104	.088	.155
		(.117)	(.131)	(.174)		(.156)	(.171)	(.256)

Table C.6 / *(Continued)*

	White Males				Black Males			
	1	2	3	4	1	2	3	4
Would Hire								
GED/Gov. Trainee	—	.031	−.009	−.389*	—	.293*	.174	.563
		(.146)	(.162)	(.247)		(.221)	(.246)	(.412)
Criminal	—	.007	−.092	−.075	—	.234*	.113	.139
		(.108)	(.118)	(.162)		(.174)	(.162)	(.236)
Short-Term, Part-Time Only	—	−.199**	−.062	−.223*	—	−.025	.003	.105
		(.111)	(.121)	(.155)		(.155)	(.172)	(.237)
Interview—Yes	—	−.141	−.068	−.041	—	−.272*	−.299*	−.017
		(.151)	(.165)	(.224)		(.204)	(.224)	(.333)
Interview—Looks For								
Motivation	—	.157*	.069	−.060	—	−.105	−.069	−.171
		(.119)	(.130)	(.174)		(.156)	(.171)	(.250)
Politeness	—	−.179*	−.151	−.109	—	−.263*	−.304*	−.078
		(.136)	(.151)	(.213)		(.184)	(.206)	(.319)
Verbal/English	—	−.175*	−.120	.028	—	−.081	.123	.082
		(.127)	(.140)	(.192)		(.173)	(.191)	(.281)
Appearance/Neatness	—	−.338**	−.300**	−.399**	—	.078	.131	.094
		(.112)	(.125)	(.169)		(.161)	(.179)	(.267)
Test								
Work Sample/Other	—	−.272**	−.210*	−.195	—	−.534**	−.564**	−.338
		(.120)	(.130)	(.268)		(.182)	(.210)	(.285)
Physical	—	.140	−.012	−.023	—	.877**	.670**	.887*
		(.156)	(.175)	(.235)		(.204)	(.237)	(.332)
Check Ed./Crim. Record	—	−.125	−.065	.068	—	.353**	.252*	.016
		(.104)	(.117)	(.159)		(.145)	(.164)	(.238)
Occupation	—	—	yes	yes	—	—	yes	yes
Industry	—	—	yes	yes	—	—	yes	yes
Seasonal/Temp.	—	—	−.065	−.063	—	—	.269	.451*
			(.191)	(.258)			(.248)	(.342)
Collective Barg.	—	—	.366**	.309	—	—	.087	−.163
			(.187)	(.257)			(.235)	(.353)
Size								
1–20 employees	—	—	.287*	.119	—	—	−.928**	−1.092*
			(.209)	(.291)			(.278)	(.392)
21–50 employees	—	—	.042	.020	—	—	−.741**	−.933*
			(.221)	(.307)			(.286)	(.421)
51–100 employees	—	—	−.110	−.128	—	—	−.570**	−.818*
			(.233)	(.333)			(.295)	(.426)
101–500 employees	—	—	−.195	−.229	—	—	−.298	−.845*
			(.204)	(.298)			(.242)	(.383)
% Applicants Black (Male/Female)	—	—	—	−.417	—	—	—	3.242*
				(.361)				(.433)
% Customers Black	—	—	—	−1.235**	—	—	—	1.180*
				(.410)				(.480)
Log L	−1372	−1282	−1097	−628	−794	−746	−627	−314
N	2633	2555	2308	1348	2633	2555	2308	1341

	White Females				Black Females			
	1	2	3	4	1	2	3	4
Would Hire								
GED/Gov. Trainee	—	−.162	−.070	.087	—	−.303*	.284*	.039
		(.142)	(.158)	(.253)		(.199)	(.220)	(.383)
Criminal	—	.056	.183*	.307**	—	−.127	−.067	−.085
		(.107)	(.120)	(.168)		(.148)	(.162)	(.233)
Short-Term, Part-Time Only	—	.035	−.016	.072	—	.171	.037	−.126
		(.109)	(.120)	(.156)		(.151)	(.164)	(.223)
Interview—Yes	—	.551**	.463**	.476**	—	−.132	−.154	−.171
		(.168)	(.187)	(.259)		(.208)	(.233)	(.363)
Interview—Looks For								
Motivation	—	−.136	−.054	−.036	—	−.015	.078	.184
		(.117)	(.129)	(.178)		(.157)	(.110)	(.250)
Politeness	—	.255**	.230*	.024	—	.077	.025	.143
		(.147)	(.165)	(.233)		(.200)	(.217)	(.330)
Verbal/English	—	.447**	.356**	.539**	—	.286*	.189	.238
		(.135)	(.152)	(.215)		(.185)	(.202)	(.300)
Appearance/Neatness	—	.140**	.076	.232*	—	.074	−.003	−.324
		(.107)	(.119)	(.069)		(.149)	(.163)	(.240)
Test								
Work Sample/Other	—	.331**	.258**	.122	—	.114	.093	.194
		(.111)	(.123)	(.164)		(.154)	(.170)	(.237)
Physical	—	−.566**	−.246*	−.762**	—	.051	.054	−.228
		(.155)	(.177)	(.264)		(.197)	(.224)	(.336)
Check Ed./Crim. Record	—	−.144*	−.100	−.104	—	.216*	.142	−.196
		(.100)	(.114)	(.158)		(.137)	(.153)	(.226)
Occupation	—	—	yes	yes	—	—	yes	yes
Industry	—	—	yes	yes	—	—	yes	yes
Seasonal/Temp.	—	—	−.265*	−.115	—	—	.358*	.113
			(.198)	(.271)			(.248)	(.365)
Collective Barg.	—	—	−.434**	−.205	—	—	−.100	−.331
			(.202)	(.269)			(.243)	(.363)
Size								
1–20 employees	—	—	.541**	.323	—	—	−.733**	−.773**
			(.202)	(.304)			(.259)	(.362)
21–50 employees	—	—	.419**	.218	—	—	−.478**	−.628*
			(.214)	(.316)			(.267)	(.391)
51–100 employees	—	—	.263	−.052	—	—	−.043	−.420
			(.229)	(.349)			(.277)	(.432)
101–500 employees	—	—	.265*	.287	—	—	−.079	−.399
			(.200)	(.308)			(.232)	(.362)
% Applicants Black (Male/Female)	—	—	—	−.697*	—	—	—	4.007**
				(.425)				(.482)
% Customers Black	—	—	—	−2.238*	—	—	—	1.680**
				(.448)				(.471)
Log L	−1438	−1329	−1112	−616	−849	−802	−686	−342
N	2633	2555	2308	1367	2633	2555	2262	1329

Appendix D: Additional Data for Chapter 5

Table D.1 / Separate Log (Wage) Equations: Coefficients (Standard Errors)

	White Males		Black Males		White Females		Black Females	
	2	4	2	4	2	4	2	4
Task								
Customers	−.063*	.011	−.024	.109	−.084**	.101*	−.000	−.012
	(.044)	(.061)	(.078)	(.140)	(.050)	(.069)	(.068)	(.106)
Read/Write	.182**	.133**	.174**	.196*	.140**	.134**	.214**	.165**
	(.041)	(.053)	(.062)	(.133)	(.038)	(.049)	(.053)	(.072)
Arithmetic	.070**	.081*	.029	−.016	−.046	−.057	.009	.091*
	(.043)	(.059)	(.069)	(.118)	(.039)	(.050)	(.048)	(.070)
Computer	−.057*	−.027	.066	.105	.241**	.120**	.073*	−.043
	(.044)	(.058)	(.071)	(.121)	(.041)	(.056)	(.052)	(.074)
Affirmative Action	.013	−.014	−.033	−.094	.039	.017	.024	−.070
	(.039)	(.053)	(.063)	(.113)	(.037)	(.047)	(.051)	(.074)
Require								
High School Diploma	.130**	.154**	.131**	.158*	.178**	.106**	.063	−.062
	(.046)	(.062)	(.067)	(.119)	(.051)	(.062)	(.064)	(.098)
General Experience	.048	.007	−.070	−.069	.037	.078*	.057	.048
	(.046)	(.062)	(.073)	(.128)	(.045)	(.057)	(.056)	(.079)
Specific Experience	.224**	.158**	.128**	.075	.115**	.022	.092*	.057
	(.046)	(.063)	(.070)	(.121)	(.042)	(.054)	(.057)	(.082)
References	−.082**	−.026	.009	.071	.017	−.002	.004	.063
	(.043)	(.061)	(.071)	(.126)	(.042)	(.054)	(.058)	(.086)
Vocational Ed./Training	.153**	.140	.085	.087	.074**	.134**	.051	.112**
	(.043)	(.059)	(.075)	(.126)	(.039)	(.048)	(.055)	(.078)

Would Hire								
GED/Gov. Training	.132**	.132*	−.007	.032	−.052	−.214**	−.653	−.072
	(.054)	(.086)	(.105)	(.255)	(.052)	(.076)	(.068)	(.113)
Criminal	.039	.040	.016	.001	.112**	.060	.081*	.070
	(.041)	(.056)	(.067)	(.111)	(.039)	(.051)	(.052)	(.075)
Short-Term, Part-Time	−.038	−.144**	−.123**	−.145**	−.090**	−.166**	−.095**	−.151**
	(.043)	(.054)	(.070)	(.104)	(.039)	(.048)	(.054)	(.071)
Interview—Yes	.063	.004	−.130*	−.053	−.087	−.067	.011	−.085
	(.058)	(.077)	(.087)	(.147)	(.068)	(.087)	(.072)	(.122)
Interview Looks For								
Appearance/Neatness	−.146**	−.106**	−.097	.105	−.080**	−.051	−.079*	−.061
	(.043)	(.058)	(.081)	(.130)	(.038)	(.048)	(.053)	(.077)
Verbal/English	−.059*	−.155**	−.072	−.280**	.027	.003	−.095*	−.095
	(.045)	(.062)	(.076)	(.133)	(.054)	(.072)	(.065)	(.086)
Politeness	−.028	−.015	−.163**	−.037	−.094**	−.049	−.140**	−.111
	(.050)	(.067)	(.084)	(.163)	(.055)	(.070)	(.075)	(.105)
Motivation	.027	.085*	.151**	.182*	.039	.036	.038	.042
	(.044)	(.066)	(.066)	(.115)	(.043)	(.055)	(.056)	(.076)
Recruiting Method								
Help-Wanted Sign	−.214**	−.215*	−.362**	−.497**	−.231**	−.094	−.070	.019
	(.109)	(.133)	(.189)	(.291)	(.094)	(.108)	(.108)	(.165)
Newspaper	−.042	.020	.067	−.045	−.004	.072	.021	.047
	(.054)	(.071)	(.101)	(.204)	(.052)	(.064)	(.081)	(.116)
Walk-In	−.163**	−.144*	−.065	−.228	−.285**	−.094	−.276**	−.060
	(.067)	(.090)	(.105)	(.195)	(.068)	(.088)	(.082)	(.116)
Current Employee	−.113**	−.055	−.034	−.178	−.081*	−.074	.020	.134
	(.055)	(.078)	(.101)	(.190)	(.056)	(.072)	(.081)	(.111)

Table D.1 / *(Continued)*

	White Males		Black Males		White Females		Black Females	
	2	4	2	4	2	4	2	4
State Employment Service	−.150*	−.123	.092	−.124	−.177	−.196	.186	.444*
	(.110)	(.147)	(.134)	(.282)	(.146)	(.188)	(.154)	(.252)
Private Employment Service	.174*	.220	.014	−.142	.091	.088	.084	.237*
	(.115)	(.188)	(.154)	(.427)	(.078)	(.106)	(.188)	(.166)
Community Agency	−.092	−.158	.180	—	.543**	.647*	.365**	.546**
	(.186)	(.340)	(.199)		(.327)	(.438)	(.205)	(.319)
School	−.004	−.155	−.132	−.300	−.158*	−.010	−.216**	.007
	(.096)	(.126)	(.193)	(.291)	(.098)	(.131)	(.120)	(.208)
Union	.648**	.453*	.725*	.405	.163	.283	.344	—
	(.203)	(.341)	(.486)	(.645)	(.234)	(.466)	(.392)	
Check Education or	−.017	−.100	−.035	−.071	.043	.052	.077*	.010
Criminal Records	(.041)	(.055)	(.070)	(.121)	(.036)	(.049)	(.049)	(.082)
Test								
Physical	−.123**	.072	.023	.025	.075	.028	.046	−.089
	(.057)	(.083)	(.098)	(.164)	(.059)	(.078)	(.071)	(.117)
Other	−.036	−.025	.122*	.053	.021	.031	.099**	.051
	(.044)	(.057)	(.089)	(.145)	(.040)	(.051)	(.058)	(.078)

Occupation	—	yes	—	yes	—	yes	—	yes
Industry	—	yes	—	yes	—	yes	—	yes
Seasonal/Temporary	—	−.027	—	−.318**	—	−.272**	—	−.298**
		(.091)		(.155)		(.094)		(.119)
Collective Bargaining	—	.190**	—	.286**	—	.021	—	.079
		(.090)		(.164)		(.088)		(.120)
Size								
1–20 employees	—	−.041	—	.090	—	−.238**	—	−.176*
		(.106)		(.176)		(.101)		(.115)
21–50 employees	—	.009	—	.084	—	−.213**	—	−.204**
		(.109)		(.204)		(.102)		(.126)
51–100 employees	—	−.073	—	.064	—	−.241**	—	−.111
101–500 employees		(.122)		(.183)		(.110)		(.129)
	—	.072	—	−.001	—	−.073	—	−.153*
		(.109)		(.171)		(.098)		(.106)
% of Employees Who Are	—	−.044	—	−.334**	—	−.099	—	.177**
Black		(.129)		(.189)		(.079)		(.083)
% of Customers Who Are	—	−.022	—	−.436**	—	.137	—	−.206*
Black		(.156)		(.251)		(.150)		(.128)
R^2	.437	.531	.353	.607	.428	.596	.593	.775
$\bar{R}^2$	.394	.430	.229	.309	.393	.526	.525	.650
N	578	358	257	145	721	432	789	177

*Represents significant results at the .20 level.
**Represents significant results at the .10 level in a two-tailed test.

References

Abraham, Katherine, and James Medoff. 1982. "Unemployment, Unsatisfied Demand for Labor, and Compensation Growth, 1956–80." In *Workers, Jobs and Inflation*, ed. M. Baily. Washington, D.C.: Brookings.

Abraham, Katherine. 1983. "Structural-Frictional v. Demand-deficient Unemployment." *American Economic Review* 73: 708–724.

Anderson, Patricia, and Bruce Meyer. 1994. "The Extent and Consequences of Job Turnover." *Brookings Papers on Economic Activity—Microeconomics*, 177–248.

Bailey, Thomas. 1990. "Changes in the Nature and Structure of Work: Implications for Skill Requirements and Skill Formation." Unpublished paper. National Center for Research on Vocational Education, University of California, Berkeley.

Ballen, John, and Richard Freeman. 1986. "Transitions between Employment and Nonemployment." In *The Black Youth Nonemployment Crisis*, ed. R. Freeman and H. Holzer. Chicago: University of Chicago Press.

Bane, Mary Jo, and David Ellwood. 1994. *Welfare Realities*. Cambridge: Harvard University Press.

Barron, John, John Bishop and William Dunkelberg. 1985. "Employer Search: The Interviewing and Hiring of New Employees." *Review of Economics and Statistics* 57: 43–52.

Barron, John, Mark Berger and Dan Black. 1994. "Employer Search,

Training, and Vacancy Duration." Unpublished paper. University of Kentucky.

Bartel, Ann, and Frank Lichtenberg. 1987. "The Comparative Advantage of Educated Workers in Implementing New Technology." *Review of Economics and Statistics* 69: 1–11.

Barton, Paul, and Irwin Kirsch. 1990. "Workplace Competencies: The Need to Improve Literacy and Employment Readiness." U.S. Department of Education, Office of Educational Research and Improvement.

Becker, Gary. 1971. *The Economics of Discrimination*. Chicago: University of Chicago Press.

Bendick, Marc, Charles Jackson and Victor Reinoso. 1994. "Measuring Employment Discrimination Through Controlled Experiments." *Review of Black Political Economy* 23: 25–48.

Bergmann, Barbara. 1971. "The Effect on White Incomes of Discrimination in Employment." *Journal of Political Economy* 79: 294–313.

Berman, Eli, John Bound and Zvi Griliches. 1994. "Changes in the Demand for Skilled Labor Within U.S. Manufacturing: Evidence from the Annual Survey of Manufacturers." *Quarterly Journal of Economics* 109: 367–397.

Bishop, John. 1993. "Improving Job Matches in the U.S. Labor Market." *Brookings Papers on Economic Activity—Microeconomics* 1: 335–390.

Bishop, John, and Mark Montgomery. 1993. "Does the Targeted Jobs Tax Credit Create Jobs at Subsidized Firms?" *Industrial Relations* 32: 289–306.

Blackburn, McKinley, and David Neumark. 1993. "Omitted Ability Bias and the Increase in Returns to Schooling." *Journal of Labor Economics* 11: 521–544.

Blanchard, Olivier, and Peter Diamond. 1989. "The Beveridge Curve." *Brookings Papers on Economic Activity* 1: 1–60.

Blanchard, Olivier, and Lawrence Katz. 1992. "Regional Evolutions." *Brookings Papers on Economic Activity* 1: 1–61.

Blanchflower, David, and Andrew Oswald. 1990. "The Wage Curve." *Scandinavian Journal of Economics* 92: 215–235.

Blank, Rebecca. 1990. "Understanding Part-Time Work." In *Research in Labor Economics* vol 11, ed. L. Bassi and D. Crawford. Greenwich, Conn.: JAI Press.

———. 1995. "Outlook for the U.S. Labor Market and Prospects for Low-Wage Entry Jobs." In *The Work Alternative: Welfare Reform and Realities in the Job Market*, ed. D. Nightingale and R. Haveman. Washington, D.C.: Urban Institute Press.

Blau, Francine, and Lawrence Kahn. 1994. "Rising Wage Inequality and the U.S. Gender Gap." *American Economic Review* 84: 23–28.

Blinder, Alan. 1973. "Wage Discrimination: Reduced-Form and Structural Estimates." *Journal of Human Resources* 8: 436–455.

Bloch, Farrell. 1994. *Antidiscrimination Law and Minority Employment.* Chicago: University of Chicago Press.

Borjas, George, Richard Freeman and Lawrence Katz. 1992. "On the Labor Market Effects of Immigration and Trade." In *Immigration and the Workforce: Economic Consequences for the United States and Source Areas*, ed. G. Borjas and R. Freeman. Chicago: University of Chicago Press.

Borjas, George, and Valerie Ramey. 1994. "Time-Series Evidence on the Sources of Trends in Wage Inequality." *American Economic Review* 84: 10–16.

Bound, John, and Richard Freeman. 1992. "What Went Wrong? The Erosion of Relative Earnings and Employment for Blacks." *Quarterly Journal of Economics* 107: 201–232.

Bound, John, and Harry Holzer. 1993. "Industrial Structure, Skill Levels, and the Labor Market for Whites and Blacks." *The Review of Economics and Statistics* 75: 387–396.

———. 1995. "Structural Changes, Employment Outcomes, and Population Adjustments: 1980–1990." Discussion paper, Institute for Research on Poverty, University of Wisconsin.

Brown, Charles, James Hamilton and James Medoff. 1990. *Employers Large and Small.* Cambridge, Mass.: Harvard University Press.

Burtless, Gary. 1985. "Are Targeted Wage Subsidies Harmful? Evidence from a Wage Voucher Experiment." *Industrial and Labor Relations Review* 39: 105–114.

———. 1995. "The Employment Prospects of Welfare Recipients." In *The Work Alternative*, ed. D. Nightingale and R. Haveman.

Cain, Glen. 1986. "The Economic Analysis of Labor Market Discrimination: A Survey." In *Handbook of Labor Economics*, ed. O. Ashenfelter and R. Layard. Amsterdam: North-Holland.

Cameron, Stephen, and James Heckman. 1993. "The Nonequivalence of High School Equivalents." *Journal of Labor Economics* 11: 1–47.

Card, David. 1990. "The Impact of the Mariel Boatlift on the Miami Labor Market." *Industrial and Labor Relations Review* 43: 245–257.

Card, David, and Thomas Lemieux. 1994. "Changing Wage Structure and Black-White Wage Differentials." *American Economic Review* 84: 29–33.

Card, David, and Alan Krueger. 1994. "Minimum Wages and Employment: A Case Study of the Fast-Food Industry in New Jersey and Pennsylvania." *American Economic Review* 84: 772–888.

Clark, Kim, and Lawrence Summers. 1981. "Demographic Differences in Cyclical Employment Variation." *Journal of Human Resources* 16: 61–79.

———. 1982. "The Dynamics of Youth Unemployment." In *The Youth Labor Market Problem: Its Nature, Causes and Consequences*, ed. R. Freeman and D. Wise. Chicago: University of Chicago Press.

Corcoran, Mary, Linda Datcher and Greg J. Duncan. 1980. "Most Workers Find Jobs Through Word of Mouth." *Monthly Labor Review* 103: 33–35.

Cross, Harry, Genevieve Kenney, Jane Mell and Wendy Zimmerman. 1990. *Employer Hiring Practices: Differential Treatment of Hispanic and Anglo Job Seekers*. Washington, D.C.: Urban Institute.

Danziger, Sheldon. 1989. "Fighting Poverty and Reducing Welfare Dependency." In *Welfare Policy for the 1990's*, ed. P. Cottingham and D. Ellwood. Cambridge: Harvard University Press.

Danziger, Sheldon, and Daniel Weinberg. 1994. "The Historical Record: Trends in Income Inequality and Poverty." In *Confronting Poverty*, ed. S. Danziger, G. Sandefur and D. Weinberg. Cambridge: Harvard University Press.

Danziger, Sheldon, and Peter Gottschalk. 1995. *America Unequal*. New York: Russell Sage Foundation.

Davidson, Carl. 1990. *Recent Developments in the Theory of Involuntary Unemployment*. Kalamazoo, Mich.: W.E. Upjohn Institute for Employment Research.

Davis, Steve, and John Haltiwanger. 1990. "Gross Job Creation and Destruction: Microeconomic Evidence and Macroeconomic Implications." In *NBER Macroeconomics Annual*. Cambridge, Mass.: MIT Press.

Devine, Theresa, and Nicholas Kiefer. 1991. *Empirical Labor Economics in the Search Framework*. Oxford: Oxford University Press.

Ellwood, David. 1982. "Teenage Unemployment: Permanent Scars or Temporary Blemishes?" In *The Youth Labor Market Problem*, ed. R. Freeman and D. Wise.

Employment and Training Institute. 1994. "Survey of Job Openings in the Milwaukee Metropolitan Area: Week of October 25, 1993." University of Wisconsin at Milwaukee.

Farley, Reynolds, Harry Holzer and Sheldon Danziger. 1995. *Detroit Divided: Racial Differences in Housing and Employment*. Unpublished paper. University of Michigan.

Feldstein, Martin. 1973. "The Economics of the New Unemployment." *The Public Interest* 33: 3–42.

Ferguson, Ronald, and Randall Filer. 1986. "Do Better Jobs Make Better Workers? Absenteeism from Work Among Inner-City Black Youths." In *Black Youth Nonemployment,* ed. R. Freeman and H. Holzer.

Ferguson, Ronald. 1993. "New Evidence on the Growing Value of Skill and Consequences for Racial Disparity and Returns to Schooling." Unpublished paper. Harvard University.

Fernandez, Roberto. 1991. "Social Isolation and the Underclass." Unpublished paper. Northwestern University.

Fix, Michael, and Raymond Struyk. 1993. *Clear and Convincing Evidence.* (Washington, D.C.: American Enterprise Institute Press, 1993).

Freeman, Richard B. 1991. "Employment and Earnings of Disadvantaged Young Men in Labor Shortage Economy." In *The Urban Underclass,* ed. C. Jencks and P. Peterson. Washington, D.C.: Brookings.

———. 1992. "Crime and the Employment of Disadvantaged Youths." In *Urban Labor Markets and Job Opportunities,* ed. G. Peterson and W. Vroman. Washington, D.C.: Urban Institute Press.

Freeman, Richard B., and James Medoff. 1984. *What Do Unions Do?* New York: Basic Books.

Freeman, Richard B., and Harry Holzer. 1986. *The Black Youth Employment Crisis.* Chicago: University of Chicago Press.

Freeman, Richard B., and Lawrence Katz. 1988. "Industrial Wage and Employment Determination in an Open Economy." In *Immigration, Trade and the Labor Market,* ed. R. Freeman. Chicago: University of Chicago Press.

Frey, William, and Reynolds Farley. 1993. "Latino, Asian and Black Segregation in Multi-Ethnic Metro Areas: Findings from the 1990 Census." Population Studies Center, University of Michigan.

Granovetter, Mark. 1974. *Getting a Job: A Study of Contacts and Careers.* Cambridge: Harvard University Press.

Grogger, Jeffrey. 1993. "The Effects of Arrests on the Employment and Earnings of Young Men." Unpublished paper. University of California, Santa Barbara.

Groshen, Erica. 1991. "Sources of Intraindustry Wage Dispersion: How Much Do Employees Matter?" *Quarterly Journal of Economics* 106: 869–884.

Gunderson, Morley. 1989. "Male-Female Wage Differentials and Policy Responses." *Journal of Economic Literature* 27: 46–72.

Hamermesh, Daniel. 1993. *Labor Demand.* Princeton: Princeton University Press.

Hauser, Robert, and Hanam Samuel Phang. 1993. "Trends in High School Dropout Among White, Black and Hispanic Youth: 1973 to 1989." Institute for Research on Poverty Discussion Paper.

Haveman, Robert. 1988. *Starting Even.* New York: Simon and Schuster.

Heckman, James. 1979. "Sample Selection Bias as Specification Error." *Econometrica* 47: 153–161.

Heckman, James, and Brook Payner. 1989. "Determining the Impact of Federal Antidiscrimination Policy on the Economic Status of Blacks." *American Economic Review* 79: 138–177.

Hirsch, Barry, and David MacPherson. 1994. "Wages, Racial Composition and Quality Sorting in Labor Markets." Unpublished paper. Florida State University.

Hollenbeck, Kevin, and Richard Willke. 1991. "The Employment and Earnings Impacts of the Targeted Jobs Tax Credit. W.E. Upjohn Institute for Employment Research.

Holzer, Harry. 1986. "Reservation Wages and their Labor Market Effects for White and Black Youth." *Journal of Human Resources* 21: 157–177.

———. 1987a. "Hiring Procedures in the Firm: Their Economic Determinants and Outcomes." In *Human Resources and Firm Performance,* ed. R. Block *et al.* Madison, Wis.: Industrial Relations Research Association.

———. 1987b. "Informal Job Search and Black Youth Unemployment." *American Economic Review* 77: 446–452.

———. 1988. "Search Methods Used by Unemployed Youth." *Journal of Labor Economics* 6: 1–12.

———. 1990a. "Wages, Employer Costs, and Employee Performance in the Firm. *Industrial and Labor Relations Review* 43: S147–S164.

———. 1990b. "The Determinants of Employee Productivity and Earnings: Some New Evidence." *Industrial Relations* 29: 403–422.

———. 1991. "The Spatial Mismatch Hypothesis: What Has the Evidence Shown?" *Urban Studies* 28: 105–122.

———. 1993. "Structural-Frictional and Demand-Deficient Unemployment in Local Labor Markets." *Industrial Relations* 32: 307–327.

———. 1994a. "Job Vacancy Rates in the Firm: An Empirical Analysis." *Economica* 61: 17–36.

———. 1994b. "Black Employment Problems: New Evidence, Old Questions." *Journal of Policy Analysis and Management* 13: 699–722.

Holzer, Harry, Lawrence Katz and Alan Krueger. 1991. "Job Queues and Wages." *Quarterly Journal of Economics* 106: 739–768.

Holzer, Harry, and Wayne Vroman. 1992. "Mismatches and the Urban Labor Market." In *Urban Labor Markets,* ed. G. Peterson and W. Vroman.

Holzer, Harry, Keith Ihlanfeldt and David Sjoquist. 1994. "Work, Search and Travel among White and Black Youth." *Journal of Urban Economics* 35: 320–345.

Hotz, V. Joseph, and Marta Tienda. 1994. "Education and Employment in a Diverse Society: Generating Inequality Through the School-to-Work Transition." Unpublished paper. University of Chicago.

Hughes, Mark, and Julie Sternberg. 1992. "The New Metropolitan Reality: Where the Rubber Meets the Road in Antipoverty Policy." Urban Institute.

Ihlanfeldt, Keith, and David Sjoquist. 1990. "Job Accessibility and Racial Differences in Youth Employment Rates." *American Economic Review* 80: 267–276.

Ihlanfeldt, Keith, and Madelyn Young. "Intrametropolitan Variation in Wage Rates: The Cast of Atlanta Fast Food Restaurant Workers." *Review of Economics and Statistics* 76: 425–433.

Johnson, James, and Melvin Oliver. 1992. "Structural Changes in the U.S. Economy and Black Male Joblessness: A Reassessment." In *Urban Labor Markets,* ed. G. Peterson and W. Vroman.

Juhn, Chinhui. 1992. "Decline of Male Labor Force Participation: The Role of Declining Market Opportunities. *Quarterly Journal of Economics* 107: 79–122.

Juhn, Chinhui, Kevin Murphy and Brook Pierce. 1993. "Wage Inequality and the Rise in the Returns to Skill." *Journal of Political Economy* 101: 410–442.

Juhn, Chinhui, Kevin Murphy and Robert Topel. 1991. "Why has the Natural Rate of Unemployment Increased Over Time?" *Brookings Papers on Economic Activity* 2: 75–142.

Kain, John. 1992. "The Spatial Mismatch Hypothesis Three Decades Later." In *Housing Policy Debate: Discrimination in the Housing and Mortgage Markets.* Fannie Mae.

Kasarda, John. 1995. "Industrial Restructuring and the Changing Location of Jobs." In *State of the Union,* Vol. 1, ed. R. Farley. New York: Russell Sage Foundation.

Katz, Lawrence. 1986. "Efficiency Wages: A Partial Evaluation." In *NBER Macroeconomics Annual,* ed. Stanley Fischer.

Katz, Lawrence, and Kevin Murphy. 1992. "Changes in Relative Wages, 1963–87: The Role of Supply and Demand Factors." *Quarterly Journal of Economics* 107: 35–78.

Kenney, Genevieve, and Douglas Wissoker. 1994. "An Analysis of the Correlates of Discrimination Facing Young Hispanic Job-Seekers." *American Economic Review* 84: 674–683.

Killingsworth, Mark. 1990. *The Economics of Comparable Worth.* W.E. Upjohn Institute for Employment Research.

Kirschenman, Joleen. 1991. "Gender Within Race in the Labor Market." Unpublished paper. University of Chicago.

Kirschenman, Joleen, and Katherine Neckerman. 1991. "We'd Love to Hire Them But . . ." In *The Urban Underclass,* ed. C. Jencks and P. Peterson.

Krueger, Alan, and Lawrence Summers. 1987. "Reflections on the Inter-Industry Wage Structure." In *Unemployment and the Structure of Labor Markets,* ed. K. Lang and J. Leonard. New York: Basil Blackwell.

Krueger, Alan. 1993. "How Computers Have Changed the Wage Structure: Evidence from Microdata, 1984–1989." *Quarterly Journal of Economics* 108: 33–60.

Lalonde, Robert, and Robert Topel. 1988. "Labor Market Adjustments to Increased Immigration." In *Immigration, Trade and the Labor Market,* ed. R. Freeman.

Lawrence, Robert, and Matthew Slaughter. 1993. "International Trade and American Wages in the 1980s: Giant Sucking Sound or Small Hiccup?" *Brookings Papers on Economic Activity—Microeconomics* 2: 161–210.

Lehman, Jeffrey. 1994. "Updating Urban Policy." In *Confronting Poverty,* ed. S. Danziger, G. Sandefur and D. Weinberg.

Leonard, Jonathan. 1990. "The Impact of Affirmative Action Regulation and Equal Opportunity Law on Black Employment." *Journal of Economic Perspectives* 4: 47–63.

Levy, Frank, and Richard Murnane. 1992. "U.S. Earning Levels and Earnings Inequality: A Review of Recent Trends and Proposed Explanations." *Journal of Economic Literature* 30: 1332–1381.

Madden, Janice. 1985. "Urban Wage Gradients: Empirical Evidence." *Journal of Urban Economics* 18: 291–301.

Mare, Robert. 1995. "Changes in Educational Attainment and School Enrollment." In *State of the Union,* Vol. 1, ed. R. Farley.

Massey, Douglas, and Nancy Denton. 1992. *American Apartheid.* Cambridge: Harvard University Press.

Maynard, Rebecca. 1995. "Subsidized Employment and Non-Labor Market Alternatives for Welfare Recipients." In *The Work Alternative.*

Mead, Lawrence. 1992. *The New Politics of Poverty*. New York: Basic Books.

Meyer, Robert, and David Wise. 1982. "High School Preparation and Early Labor Force Experience." In *The Youth Labor Market Problem*, ed. R. Freeman and D. Wise.

Mincer, Jacob. 1966. "Comment On Holt and David." In *The Measurement of Interpretation of Job Vacancies*. New York: National Bureau of Economic Research.

Moffitt, Robert. 1992. "Incentive Effects of the U.S. Welfare System." *Journal of Economic Literature* 30: 1–61.

Montgomery, James. 1991. "Social Networks and Labor Market Outcomes: Toward an Economic Analysis." *American Economic Review* 81: 1408–1418.

Moss, Phil, and Chris Tilly. 1991. "Why Black Men are Doing Worse in the Labor Market: A Review of Supply-Side and Demand-Side Explanations." Social Science Research Council.

Moss, Phil, and Chris Tilly. 1993. "Soft Skills and Race." Unpublished. University of Massachusetts at Lowell.

Murnane, Richard. 1993. "The Returns to the GED Reconsidered." Unpublished. Harvard University.

Murnane, Richard, John Willett and Frank Levy. 1995. "The Growing Importance of Cognitive Skills in Wage Determination." Working Paper, National Bureau of Economic Research.

Neal, Derek, and William Johnson, 1994. "The Role of Pre-Market Factors in Black-White Wage Differences." Unpublished. University of Chicago.

Neumark, David, and William Wascher. 1992. "Employment Effects of Minimum and Subminimum Wages: Panel Data on State Minimum Wage Laws." *Industrial and Labor Relations Review* 46: 55–81.

Newman, Katherine, and Chauncy Lennon. 1995. "Finding Work in the Inner City: How Hard Is It Now? How Hard Will It Be for the AFDC Recipients?" Unpublished. Columbia University.

New York City Department of Employment. 1994. "New York City Employer Survey: Summary Report." August.

Oaxaca, Ronald. 1973. "Male-Female Wage Differentials in Urban Labor Markets." *International Economic Review* 14: 693–709.

O'Neill, June. 1990. "The Role of Human Capital in Earnings Differences Between White and Black Men." *Journal of Economic Perspectives* 4: 25–45.

Packer, Arnold, and John Wirt. 1992. "Changing Skills of the U.S.

Workforce: Trends of Supply and Demand." In *Urban Labor Markets*, ed. G. Peterson and W. Vroman.

Papke, Leslie. 1993. "What Do We Know about Enterprise Zones?" National Bureau of Economic Research Working Paper No. 4251, January.

Parsons, Donald. 1986. "The Employment Relationship: Job Attachment, Work Effort, and the Nature of Contracts." In *Handbook of Labor Economics*, ed. O. Ashenfelter and R. Layard.

Pedder, Sophie. 1991. "Social Isolation and the Labour Market: Black Americans in Chicago." Unpublished paper. University of Chicago.

Pissarides, Christopher. 1985. "Short-Run Equilibrium Dynamics of Unemployment, Vacancies, and Real Wages." *American Economic Review* 75: 676–690.

Rees, Albert. 1966. "Information Networks in Labor Markets." *American Economic Review* 56: 559–566.

Revenga, Ana. 1992. "Exporting Jobs: The Impact of Import Competition on Employment and Wages in U.S. Manufacturing." *Quarterly Journal of Economics* 107: 255–284.

Rich, Lauren. 1994. "The Long-Run Impact of Early Nonemployment: A Reexamination." Unpublished paper. University of Michigan.

Rivera-Batiz, Francisco. 1992. "Quantitative Literacy and the Likelihood of Employment Among Young Adults in the U.S." *Journal of Human Resources* 27: 318–328.

Rosen, Sherwin. 1986. "The Theory of Equalizing Differences." In *Handbook of Labor Economics*, ed. O. Ashenfelter and R. Layard.

Rosenbaum, James, and Susan Popkin. 1991. "Employment and Earnings of Low-Income Blacks Who Move to Middle-Class Suburbs." In *The Urban Underclass*, ed. C. Jencks and P. Peterson.

Sachs, Jeffrey, and Howard Shatz. 1994. "Trade and Jobs in U.S. Manufacturing." *Brookings Papers on Economic Activity* 1: 1–84.

Secretary's Commission on Achieving Necessary Skills. 1991. *What Work Requires of Schools*. U.S. Department of Labor.

Sider, Hal. 1985. "Unemployment Duration and Incidence: 1968–82." *American Economic Review* 75: 461–472.

Smith, James, and Finis Welch. 1989. "Black Economic Progress After Myrdal." *Journal of Economic Literature* 27: 519–564.

Sorensen, Elaine. 1994. *Comparable Worth: Is It a Worthy Policy?* Princeton: Princeton University Press.

Spence, Michael. 1973. "Job Market Signalling." *Quarterly Journal of Economics* 87: 355–374.

Stanback, Thomas, and Richard Knight. 1976. *Suburbanization and the City*. New York: Columbia University Press.

Thurow, Lester. 1979. *Generating Inequality*. Cambridge: Harvard University Press.

U.S. Department of Labor. 1993. "High Performance Work Practices and Firm Performance." Unpublished paper.

Wacquant, Loic, and William Wilson. 1989. "Poverty, Joblessness, and the Social Transformation of the Inner City." In *Welfare Policy*, ed. P. Cottingham and D. Ellwood.

Waldinger, Roger. 1987. "Changing Ladders and Musical Chairs: Ethnicity and Opportunity in Post-Industrial New York." *Politics and Society*. 15: 369–401.

Wilson, William. 1987. *The Truly Disadvantaged*. Chicago: University of Chicago Press.

Zax, Jeffrey. 1991. "Compensation for Commutes in Labor and Housing Markets." *Journal of Urban Economics* 30: 192–207.

Index

Boldface numbers refer to figures and tables.